The American Presidency

The Kenyan Candidate & Modern Presidents' Brilliance and Blunders

by

James Grey Johns

authorHOUSE®

AuthorHouse™
1663 Liberty Drive, Suite 200
Bloomington, IN 47403
www.authorhouse.com
Phone: 1-800-839-8640

First published by AuthorHouse 10/8/2008

ISBN: 978-1-4389-2266-9 (sc)

Library of Congress Control Number: 2008909114

Printed in the United States of America
Bloomington, Indiana

This book is printed on acid-free paper.

ABOUT THE AUTHOR

Author James Grey Johns writes and comments about a variety of subjects under different pen names, covering speeches and presentations, finance, business, politics, the environment, and family issues, in the forms of articles, newsletters, booklets, and participation on cable television panels and radio programs.

He has traveled extensively, visiting over 35 of the states, and, he has lived in California, Connecticut, Florida, New York, and Virginia. Johns, who has seen military service, has worked with persons in The White House and in Legislatures, and State Judiciaries, with officials in foreign countries in Europe, Asia, Africa, and South America.

ACKNOWLEDGEMENTS

Mindful of the privacy offered by anonymity, special thanks to Marlene and Bill S., my favorite editor Paul R. M., my favorite attorney Ira L. S., my favorite businessman Brian D. P., and all those others who have been inspirational and who provided support and encouragement, without whose efforts this book would not have been written.

INTRODUCTION

A number of 'awakening' events led to this work. I was a small-l liberal inclined to favor Democrats during my college days and in the years that followed. Balance and fair play, rooting for the underdog, harmony, were my hallmarks. I was a keen history buff, and, I tried to keep up with current events. My favorite Presidents were Harry S. Truman and Hubert H. Humphrey. I was taken in by the style of JFK, taken aback by the dark visage of Richard Nixon, admired the skills of LBJ. I was fanatical about the civil rights movement, was an early, direct supporter of women's rights, thought ill of South Africa during its apartheid days, and was naïve about communism. Bottom line: I perceived Democrats as being 'for the people', and Republicans as indifferent, cynical, overly conservative, not caring. The media, print and electronic, was my lodestar, along with Hollywood 'message' films.

As I matured, I started to appreciate the importance of substance over style, of practicality over idealism, of credibility, of integrity, and I began to question what Democrat politicians and policies were accomplishing. I read a book by Reeves, "President Kennedy", which provided a whole new look at JFK, his lies, indecision, womanizing, evasions, and so much that was duplicitous. I heard a speech by Irving Kristol, a neo-conservative figure, which added to my growing doubts about liberalism and awakened me to the virtues of conservatism. I started reading THE WALL STREET JOURNAL regularly, and found it to be informative, balanced, objective, and superbly edited. In contrast, I realized that THE NEW YORK TIMES was subjective, imbalanced, increasingly biased, agenda-driven, and partisan. With thanks to Don Imus, who was the first to pull me away from morning television and onto Talk Radio, which was much more informative and factual. I learned to appreciate Rush, Sean, Mark,

Steve, Laura, John, and many other radio hosts. Publications such as NewsMax, Imprimus, The New York Sun, The New York Post, became my mini-Bibles –but first and foremost was the JOURNAL, without whose articles and editorials this book would never have seen the light.

At first I just wanted to compare modern Presidents by one litmus. I did not originally intend to write a polemic. Early in 2008, I tried be objective and fact-driven, not emotional, about the Democrats and their standard bearers, Obama and Clinton. It became clear that the Democrat Party put Power over both Principle and the national interest, that Obama, so lacking, so wrong in so many vital areas, is a danger to America's very survival. That's the way I called it.

PART I – THE KENYAN

CANDIDATE

OBAMA IN HIS OWN WORDS…

"Should the political winds shift in an ugly direction, I will stand with the Muslims."

"I found solace in nursing a pervasive sense of grievance and animosity against my mother's [white] race."

"It remained necessary to prove which side you were on, to show your loyalty to the black masses, to strike out and name names."

"I never emulate white men and brown men whose fates don't speak to **my own** [**as a black man,** *son of Africa*]."

"In 20 years of attending my church, I cannot recall hearing Reverend Wright say anything anti-American or anti-white."

"As I've said about the flag pin, I don't want to be perceived as taking sides. There are a lot of people in the world to whom the American flag is a symbol of oppression. And the anthem conveys a war-like message. You know, the bombs bursting in air and all. It should be swapped for something less parochial and less bellicose. I like the song 'I'd Like to Teach the World to Sing'. If that was our anthem, then I might salute it."

"I was only 8 years old when my friend [ultra-left admitted terrorist] William Ayers was bombing the Pentagon and police stations in America. We have worked together on boards, he raised money for me. I don't think he really meant it when he said he was sorry he hadn't bombed more places."

"I cannot support legislation letting a newborn that survived an abortion continue to live, which is why I opposed the Born Alive Infants Protection Act."

"I learned more about my African American heritage from my [*white*] mother."

"I wish I could have been at my mother's bedside [in Hawaii] when she died, but I was in the midst of my first campaign for political office [in Chicago]."

...AND A FEW FROM ME...

Republican Vice President candidate Gov. Sarah Palin is not a woman trying for a man's job. She is a more experienced and otherwise a more qualified office holder, with executive and administrative accomplishments, than either of the two men, both strictly lawyer-legislators on the Democrat ticket.

POSITION WANTED:

Conservative Republican; early 40s; Governor; hunter; Pro-the average citizen, against corrupt practices; married w/ 5 children; seeks U.S. Vice Presidency. Contact: (a) Teddy Roosevelt; (b) Sarah Palin; (c) either.

YOUR VOTE

Don't let the biased, agenda-driven major media and pollsters, nor irrational emotion disenfranchise you. You yourself have more than enough sense to figure out whom to vote for. Your only 'special interest' is what you believe is best for you and who else and whatever else counts such as your family, job, business, etc. Look behind what ambitious politicians say and biased journalists write and telecast, to separate fiction, demagogy, and empty promises from undeniable facts and substance.

TOP OF THE TICKET

One candidate, McCain, is a patriot, a hero, a maverick that has a record of working both sides of the aisle, and years of experience in different capacities. The other, Obama, hasn't even produced a Certified Birth Certificate, stresses what he thinks is wrong with

America, has kept to the extreme left side of his aisle, has no executive experience nor any legislative accomplishments, has a history of associating with black racists, terrorists and anarchists, and corrupt political and business interests.

WHICH IS BETTER?

Better a cowboy than a coward.

IF ONLY...

If only the Democrats were willing to fight terrorists as hard as they've been fighting George Bush, we would all be better off,

SOOO GOOD

Gov. Sarah Palin is so good, I wish I could vote twice for the ticket.

LET...

To: Pelosi, Reid, Obama -- LET US DRILL! LET US DRILL! LET US DRILL!

The Bakken Formation in and around the Dakotas, alone has over 500 billion barrels of oil, worth trillions, which at market will reduce costs to about $16 a barrel – that's the level before the OPEC embargo of the 1970s. Inside and around our borders there actually is more recoverable oil than in Saudi Arabia. Recoverable shale oil in Colorado, Utah, and Wyoming are estimated to be over 1 trillion barrels. Recoverable natural gas resources in Alaska, off our coasts, and in parts of the American West, are put at over 600 trillion cubic feet. Recoverable oil estimates from Alaska, the coasts, and elsewhere in the U.S., if drilling were permitted, would yield generations of inexpensive energy.

For the sake of Americans and America, stop the parliamentary tricks, Nancy and Harry, and allow an up-or-down vote.

INTEGRITY, CREDIBILITY, ABILITY ARE OWED THE PEOPLE.

In November, Americans go to the polls to vote for those leaders that will take on the duties, responsibilities, challenges, and problems our nation faces. In January, the political leadership of our country will change. But, instead of listening to vague and pie-in-the-sky promises and ideas, the unceasing, non-factual, emotion-based finger-pointing blame, the attempts to weasel out of so-called 'misspeaks', false hopes, the people are entitled to much better.   Here is what I think most sensible American men and women expect of the candidates: People who can be trusted to put the national interest over their personal interests; People who will use non-partisanship and genuine bipartisanship, rather than the quest for political party advantage and exploitation, to get needed things done promptly and well, for the greater good; People whose principles are put before their raw ambition; People who have demonstrated they can work with Congressional men and women from the other side of the aisle, and, others in the broad political spectrum – and not just make empty claims about that, when their records show otherwise.   How can a person with a thin record that also is the most one-sided (liberal in this case) in the entire Senate, expect voters to ignore that, or, accept the notion of bipartisanship? Mere celebrity, good looks, youth, clever speaking abilities, being the darling of the media, are not substitutes for the capabilities for the highest office on the land. I find it curious in that in one breath candidate Obama says "we live in the greatest nation in the history of the world", and then in the next he promises to change that! Probably, but not for the better.

Our nation needs people who will defend America and Americans, strive to really advance our economy for the sake of people and growth, and promote our shared interests. People with actual experience – in business, in government, in the military. You dare not place a promising, stylish and articulate high-school quarter-back to start in the Super Bowl -- unless you want to lose. It is easy to make promises – the hard part is delivering them. What is worse is making promises that cannot be kept, or which come at unsupportable costs, or which are glib insincerities in the first place.

DEMOCRATS ARE SHREWDER

How clever Democrats are. They are the willing, culpable instruments that have led to record oil prices, greater dependency on foreign oil, a weaker dollar, threats to national security. Yet, with the profound, naked assistance of the major media and a good deal of academia, the Republicans are the ones being blamed for the mess. For more than a generation, Congressional Democrats, Democrat Presidents' policies, environmental extremists and their blind rigidity, judges that consider themselves above the law and above the other branches of government, are responsible for $4.00 and still-climbing gasoline prices, the weakest dollar in memory, trade deficits, and so many other ills that have befallen the nation. Don't forget to thank the tyrannical leadership of Pelosi and Reid, who have regularly abandoned democratic principles and true bipartisanship on a host of key matters, from energy policy to Social Security reform, to the Iraqi conflict. Party, power and pandering are their hallmarks, not principles or people.

With few exceptions – Zell Miller comes to mind – the Democrats have been hijacked by the left, and, seem quite comfortable with ignoring the interests of the people. There apparently aren't any Harry Trumans in that Party, with such principles as love of country, defense of the nation, genuine care for people.

DUMBER AND DUMB

Joe Biden, the 2008 Democrat Vice President nominee, has been called "The dumbest man in the Senate; still, he has some of the qualities needed to be President; He has run for that office a number of times, never getting past the primaries. Net-net, Biden is not as poorly qualified as his running mate, Barack Obama, although it should be noted neither man has any executive experience. Speaking of 'dumb', during the Olympics, Obama suggested the United States should model its infrastructure after that bastion of efficiency, safety, environmentalism, and other dubious accomplishments, Red China. China also leads the world in executions and in harvesting body parts involuntarily from so-called 'enemies of the State'. Universal Unhealthy Care?

Obama's central campaign issue: Washington is Broken (True, it was fractured by Liberal Democrats dominating the Party), and the old establishment must be swept away. Hello, Barack, Biden has been in the Senate 10 years longer than McCain. Biden was one of the few Democrat Senators to push for a surge in Iraq, alongside McCain, before Bush adopted the policy. Later on, Biden cut and ran. Along the way he proclaimed the surge would not work, that the conflict was lost, and that the only way out was to partition Iraq into three parts. Not exactly the wisdom of a Solomon.

That Democrat Convention closer in the stadium, which was fitting for a rock star concert, lacked dignity. Is there no end to the egos and elitism of the Democrats? Maybe Obama is seeking a Grammy Award, at heart...

CONVENTION

I could not help noticing one glaring omission at the 2008 Democrat Convention: Truth

HONESTY AND OPENESS

So, both Senators Obama and Biden have indicated, right out of the Modern Democrat Playbook, that they will see to it there will be more openness, transparency, and honesty in government. Sure, and the Sun really rises in the West and the Clinton's have never really lied, they just misspoke (on being found out).

But, as of early September, Obama has yet to release (he has refused, to date) the following documents:

- a Certified Birth Certificate
- a Record of his Baptism
- His medical records
- His Selective Service Registration
- Records from the following educational institutions: Columbia, Harvard, and Occidental – especially academic performance in light of benefiting from affirmative action programs, and, social behavior. McCain, in contrast, openly said he was in the very lowest portion of his graduating class, academically, and, that he was a hell-raiser in school.

As for the just plain, blue collar, working class identification of Biden, furnished by William McGurn:

- His income ranks among the top 5% of all Americans
- He lives in 'Chateau Country', in Delaware
- He left his roots in working class city Scranton in the 1950s

- Beltway Outsider? He's been in the Congress since 1972
- As a member of Congress he has one of the most generous pension plans in the nation, but, he opposes private Social Security accounts that would give a similar pension to a nurse
- The children of both Senators Biden and Obama attend upscale private schools. However, both Senators are opposed to support charter or similar schools for inner-city children (because of the opposition of teachers' unions, which are solid Democrat special interest voters).
- In fact, both Biden and Obama's idea of improving education is to give more power and funding to bureaucrats and teachers unions, whose interests they put ahead of students, instead of to parents.

FISCAL RESPONSIBILITY

(With thanks to Sen. Jim DeMint) So Obama wants to cut wasteful spending.

Hard to believe since he has requested nearly $1 billion in earmarks for pet projects since 2005. Sen. Biden of Delaware is more modest, securing about $100 million a year recently.

BIDEN THE DEPENDABLE ?

The Senator claims he is a good friend of Israel's. However, he has told the Israelis that (a) they should accept the idea of a nuclear Iran and (b) he was opposed to Israel attacking Iran's nuclear facilities – as if he could dictate policy to any sovereign nation.

Biden also suggested, some time ago, that if America gave the Iranians $200 million, the Iranians would behave peacefully.

Back during the Clinton administrations, the then-Commander-in-Chief took military action in Serbia, Haiti, and a few other places, without once seeking or obtaining Congressional approval. But, Biden is on record as saying that if President Bush bombs Iran without Congressional approval, he, Biden, would move to get Bush impeached. Can you imagine a President who cannot take action, well short of outright war (the Constitution stipulates that for war Congress must vote its approval; for action short of declaring war, Congress has no authority, other than to withhold or reduce monies for the purpose), without permission of a majority of the legislative branch? Little wonder enemy leaders want Democrats elected to the White House and controlling the Congress.

PALIN PLUSSES

In fact, as Governor, Mayor, and Councilwoman, Ms. Palin has more executive and administrative credentials than Obama, short legislative-, and Biden, long legislative-experience, combined. She has exercised her duties as the State's National Guard Commander in Chief, in natural disasters and emergencies. In addition, she has other qualities the two Senators lack: principles, sincerity, credibility, and integrity. As for foreign affairs, apart from meeting with a few foreign leaders and making speeches, what substantive and positive action has either Obama, over three years of sometime attendance in the Senate, or

Biden, a Senator since 1973, ever accomplished? Answer: Nothing at all!

In contrast, as reported in some of the press (see Palin Prevails, below) and by Alaskans Debbie and Rus Doe, Governor Palin is admired, respected, and appreciated by most Alaskans, and, enjoys an 80% approval rating. She is not "a beltway politician" or subservient to the "good old boys club", or her Party Establishment, or the major oil interests. "She doesn't wilt under pressure and will stand up for what she believes is in the best interest of the people, even when it means clashing with the legislature. She has vetoed excessive spending and after initially supporting the idea to bring federal funds to the state, reversed her stand and said 'No thank you' to the 'Bridge to Nowhere' that passed the U.S. Congress and was approved by Obama and Biden. Palin refuses to cozy up to the media, recognizing its bias and corruption. She sold the Governor's private jet, drives herself to her office, fired the mansion chef.

VEEP DUTIES

The Vice President of the United States has two basic duties as provided in the Constitution: To preside over the Senate; to be first in line for the Presidency in the event the President dies, is impeached, is incapacitated, or otherwise unable to perform the duties of that office. The President will also assign, if and as he/she chooses to do so, the Vice President to be his agent and advisor, which may entail trips to foreign lands or some responsibilities , for example, oversight of the Space program. Accordingly, a Governor has more responsibilities than the Vice President.

FDR's first Vice President Garner reportedly said that "the position wasn't worth a pitcher of spit" – however, some believe he actually said pitcher of piss, and the press cleaned it up.

TEEN-AGE PREGNANCY

So Palin's daughter Bristol got pregnant at 17. Obama's mother also got pregnant at 17 and gave birth at 18.

BIDEN'S BLUNDERS

With acknowledgement to Peter Wehner, an ethics and policy expert:

- Biden opposed giving aid to the South Vietnamese government, after the U.S. was engaged per the policies of JFK and Lyndon Johnson. He voted to cut-off funds, which resulted in the Government falling, a Communist take-over, and hundreds of thousands or more deaths.
- Biden's advocacy of massive defense cuts went well beyond what fellow liberal Democrats Muskie and Mondale would tolerate.
- Biden opposed America helping to turn back the Communist takeover attempts in Nicaragua and El Salvador.
- Biden opposed modernization of U.S. strategic nuclear forces, and, the Reagan Strategic Defense Initiative (which the latter, incidentally, led to the collapse of the Soviet Empire.
- Biden opposed the Antiballistic Missile Treaty.
- Biden voted against the first Gulf War.
- Biden initially voted for the Iraq War, then, as many Democrats did, turned tail and opposed it; he

also opposed the surge (which, as is now known, led to the collapse of the insurgency and of Al Queda in Iraq), which has brought the conflict within sight of victory.

• Obama has lambasted the foreign policy of the Bush administrations as the fault of Beltway insiders, and, has proclaimed that salvation lies with bringing in fresh ideas from the outside. Yet, his running mate, Biden, chosen for Biden's foreign policy expertise, has been a Washington insider for over 30 years, with a consistent record of being wrong time after time.

PALIN PREVAILS

As reported by Kimberly Strassel of The Wall Street Journal, Sarah Palin took on the establishment, including her own party, and prevailed. Alaska derives 85% of state revenues from the oil industry; traditionally, oil interests had a long-term sweetheart arrangement with the state's politicians such that the former got its way in matters and the latter would receive a host of rewards, including lucrative jobs after leaving office.

Then Ms. Palin, as a member of the state oil and gas regulatory agency, blew the whistle about shady, secret energy dealings, bucking the establishment in the process. She resigned, ran for Governor on a platform of transparency, competitive bidding, measures that would be in the greater interest to the citizenry, including a fairer tax arrangement – and won.

In the process then-new Governor Palin uncovered bribes and other unsavory dealings between the oil industry and top politicos. Under her leadership an ethics law was passed, oil oversight was tightened up, the tax laws were rewritten more fairly, politicians were investigated and some were convicted. Through a new risk and profit-sharing arrangement – that is not a windfall profits tax – she was able to see to it that every Alaskan will receive a $1,200 royalty check from the oil bonanza, towards lessening the pressures of higher energy prices. She is pro-drilling, the days of sweetheart deals are over, and there is a new, mutually respectful and transparent relationship between the oil industry and the political structure.

PALIN'S QUALIFICATIONS?

"…Where is it written that governors and mayors, like Dianne Feinstein of San Francisco, are too local, too provincial [to be nominated for Vice President]… Why shouldn't a little-known woman have the same opportunity to grow?" Could that possibly be about Republican Governor Palin?

Sorry, THE NEW YORK TIMES EDITORIAL, July 3, <u>1984</u>, was for the Democrats' nominating Congresswoman Geraldine Ferraro's for VP. However, showing its true colors once again, in September, 2008, the TIMES came out <u>against</u> Republican Gov. Palin, a former Mayor of a small-town in Alaska, as a little-known, too provincial, insufficiently qualified woman. Doesn't the TIMES realize some of us read and remember or save what we read?

FIRST GENTLEMAN IN WAITING

Todd Palin, husband of Gov. Palin, has previously taken off months from work to help care for their five children. A union member who works as an oil-field production operator, he laments how much natural gas – which could be a very useful energy resource for America – has to be pumped back into the ground or flared (carefully burned) off, because there isn't a completed pipeline to take the gas to market in the lower 48 states. He is part Eskimo, a tiny minority in the U.S., but none-the-less he loves his country and does not harbor grievances.

OBAMA'S CHANGES RE WORKING WOMEN, RACIAL EQUALITY

According to Economist Diana Furchgott-Roth, Obama in September spread a little lie about Gov. Palin, stating that she [of all people] is opposed to equal pay for equal work. There is something called the Equal Pay Act of 1963 which guarantees equality and which gives employees who feel they have been discriminated against, upon adequate proof, the right to sue employers, with the latter bearing the burden in Court.

Obama is pushing for a new standard, 'The Equal Pay for Equal Worth' concept, which would add onerous regulation and open matters for his friends the trial lawyers. Under that proposed standard, for example, should a home health aide receive the same as a snow-plow driver? Should a teacher's aide job, primarily but not exclusively filled by women, be paid the same as a mechanic, primarily but not exclusively filled by men? Under the Fair Pay Act of 2007 that Obama favors, he would give plaintiffs in pay-discrimination suits the capability to sue with no statute of limitations. That would create a bonanza for the Dems' favorite special interest, the plaintiffs attorneys…and if enacted it would result in employers tending not to hire women in the first place.

According to educator Bradley C.S. Watson, currently, most states require that state governments not engage in discrimination on the basis of race, sex, color, ethnicity, or national origin. These are called race neutral practices, to rebuke a 4-to-3 Supreme Court decision in 2003, which held that the purported need for diversity could justify racial preferences [for non-whites] in college admissions. The latter is approximately a code for quotas –even though it flies in the face of the 14th's Amendment Equal Protection Clause of the Constitution, and, the 'all men are created equal' language in the Declaration of Independence, and, the Civil Rights Act of 1964.

Obama has said he would take this further, to make things 'look right', by biasing toward the poor, African-Americans, gays, the disabled, and the aged – all, by the way, constituencies of the Democrats.

At minimum, these ideas would further open the door to endless lawsuits, threats of protests, product boycotts, charges of racism, homophobia, et. al., and give new currency to the Jesse Jacksons, Al Sharptons, ACLU, and their legions in the media and radical left in the U.S., to extort, intimidate, and bring the country further down by division.

CLOSING THE PAY GAP

With thanks to economics Professor Casey B. Mulligan, the record shows that women's annual wage growth compared to men's was highest in the administrations of Reagan, Bush I, and Bush II, and were minuscule in the administrations of Carter and Clinton. Those Dems talk a good case, but apparently really don't put their money where their mouths are.

CLARIFICATION

In America there is no such thing today as 'mainstream media'. With very few exceptions, the press, especially the main electronic media, positioned itself on the 'left bank' a long time ago. As for the world media, it is far worse. I frankly find many fictional novels to contain more facts than so-called news accounts.   Journalists are supposed to be objective, unbiased, non-partisan, balanced, accurate (no misinformation, no disinformation), fair, and with no agenda other than to report the news straight. Increasingly, for more than a generation, the major media has been patently biased, subjective, partisan, imbalanced, inaccurate, agenda-driven, even malicious, at the altar of liberal Democrats as they crucify Conservatives and most Republicans.   Little wonder polls show the American public rate the press barely above felons in approvals, and not much below the present Congress.

The media's inclinations are well on the side of what is or seems to be wrong, pessimism about Conservative leadership efforts and proposals, providing platforms for disingenuous liberal politicians seeking political leverage. The media plays favorites, and frequently is just plain nasty and deliberately dishonest.   Republicans, even

Republicans that happen to be African-American, can rarely do well in their eyes, Liberal Democrats rarely do wrong. Foreign media American-bashers are driven to those positions by false charges of American imperialism or accomplishment.

Europeans particularly seem to forget our nation sacrificed blood and treasure to rescue countries from Nazi Germany and later on from Soviet domination. – when we could have easily stayed on the sidelines, until America became the target for fascism and global communism. Maybe that is why in part they foolishly look to Obama as an appeaser in the mold of Chamberlain and Vichy France. Journalists need to be emphatically reminded of honest principles, and a wake-up call is needed for the shareholder-owners and executives of their companies. The declines in readership, viewers, ad revenue, reflect Americans increasingly fed up with the bias. Freedom of the press is a responsibility, not a blanket pass to violate security, put military and intelligence service men and women at risk, expose defense secrets or otherwise compromise the national interest, and ignore responsibilities for accurate economic reporting.

In the meantime, for myself, I stopped watching telecasts and broadcasts from biased electronic media, which is most of the broadcast and cable networks, (with few exceptions such as The Wall Street Journal and Fox News), buying major newspapers and magazines that also practice the same kind of biased reporting. Of course, I miss out on all those advertisers whose products and services I do not buy, because I do not watch, read, or listen to those programs which they sponsor. I prefer factual, balanced 'Talk Radio' and a handful of publications that are accuracy-driven and principled.

ENVIRONMENTAL POLICY 101

We should do what is sensible and affordable, and, respond to acute, dire situations when they occur. The rest of the agenda can wait. The planet is primarily for humans and our needs, and we are smart enough to conserve what is truly precious – which does not include some tiny fish or other creature that stands in the way of an infinitely higher priority.   We should always keep in mind what the potential impact may be on prices, jobs, dislocations, before moving ahead on some questionable quest about some unproven, fear-based notion pegged to 50 years in the future.   Environmental radicals are opportunists who realize what policies are actually intended to benefit themselves and their backers. They also know they can dupe the masses, through biased, unscientific media reporting, to go along. As much as anything else, we have to relax, by one means or another, the stranglehold radical environmentalists, especially lawyers, have on the Democrat Party, and, the favored position they have with a non-objective press.

ENVIRONMENTAL POLITICS: WET AND WILD

Despite the devastation caused by Hurricane Katrina and before the waters from 2008's Hurricaine Gustav had receded, a big federal flood-control project intended to reduce flooding in the Mississippi Delta, was shelved, owing to the work of environmentalists who argued the project would damage wildlife refuges.

UNIVERSAL HEALTH CARE?

Show me the logic: If currently 10 million medical/ health professionals take care of 200 million people in America, and you add 50 million more without a commensurate increase in the professionals, universal care will not work unless services are cut back, people are made to wait longer, the quality of care diminishes, etc. Atop those unwelcome outcomes, paying for universal health care will mean those that work and businesses will have to pay more taxes, while those that do not work will get increased care. In short, Pay More; Get Less; Face Higher Prices!

MILITARY FATALITIES: DON'T RELY ON LEFT-BANK MEDIA

If you asked someone now: during whose administration – Clinton's eight peaceful years, and Bush's seven war laden years – were there more military fatalities by any cause, the Media would lie, parse, or ignore providing an accurate answer. But, the Congressional Research Service (CRS) has published the facts. Between 1993 and 2000, 14,107 members of the military died; between 2001 and 2007, with Afghanistan and Iraq conflicts raging, there were 7,932 deaths among members of the military. The lowest amount occurred during Clinton's second watch, in 1997. The figures cover total military personnel on active duty, and include all causes from military action to terrorist incidents to accidents. From 1980 through 2007, following is the military fatalities tally – and it is hard to believe. Another myth put to rest is the misbelief that blacks and Latinos represent an inordinate percentage of military deaths. In actuality, the fatality pattern reflects the general population, with whites, in proportion and absolutely, having the most casualties, as shown in the following tabulation.

Year	Administration	Fatalities
1980	Carter (D)	2,392
1981	Reagan (R)	2,380
1982	"	2,319
1983	"	2,465
1984	"	1,999
1985	"	2,252
1986	"	1,984
1987	"	1,983
1988	"	1,819
1989	Geo. H.W. Bush(R)	1,636
1990	"	1,508
1991	"	1,787
1992	"	1,293
1993	Clinton (D)	1,213
1994	"	1,075
1995	"	2,465
1996	"	2,318
1997	"	817
1998	"	2,252
1999	"	1,984
2000	"	1,983
2001	Geo. W. Bush (R)	890
2002	"	1,007
2003	"	1,410
2004	"	1,887
2005	"	919
2006	"	920
2007	"	899

HOW TO PROLONG AND MAYBE LOSE A WAR

Follow the Democrat - Liberal Road. Just keep chipping away at a Commander-in-Chief's authority and resources to wage war against terrorists.

LOSERS AND HYPOCRITES

Democrats: We've changed our minds. We were brainwashed into supporting the war in Iraq. We want to pull out. The war is lost.

Surge? Don't be ridiculous. So what if the enemy learns when and that we are pulling out. Vietnam déjà vu?

Republicans: We stayed. The surge worked. The war is mostly won, al Qaeda is on the run. Iraq is a budding democracy, no longer under the heel of a murderous, terrorist-supporting dictator.

Then along comes that biased against Republicans author Bob Woodward. He helped torpedo Nixon, cast doubts on Reagan and George H.W. Bush,, and isn't very fond of George W. Bush. His latest book, "The War Within", is a so-called 'objective' look inside the administration , the conduct of the War, the differences with top generals. As reported by William McGurn, the Preface of his book includes remarks from General George Casey, who long thought the War was lost, opposed the surge, and otherwise undercut the Republican White House – which is just what Woodward lives for. Casey was replaced, I believe, by the much more able and patriotic Gen. David Petraeus. Another brilliant strategist Woodward used in the opening of the book was Robert McNamara, who helped lose Vietnam and on the home front helped Detroit along the path of losing its leadership of the auto industry.

AMBITION VS. DECENCY

In his memoir, "Dreams from My Father", Barack Obama stated he learned more about his African-American heritage from his American mother than from his Kenyan father. His mother, then 52 and suffering from ovarian and uterine cancer, was on her deathbed in 1995. Obama, at the time busy with his first campaign for office, <u>chose</u> not to be at her side at the time of her death. What a loving son…

As for Obama's claim as a unifier, in "Dreams' he wrote that he ceased to advertise my mother's [white] race at 12 or 13 when "I began to suspect that by doing so I was ingratiating myself to whites". Obama "found solace in nursing a pervasive sense of grievance and animosity against my mother's race."

He also wrote that "it remained necessary to prove which side you were on, to show your loyalty to the black masses, to strike out and name names".

And, "I never emulate white men and brown men whose fates don't speak to my own [as a black man, son of Africa]".

It sounds more like a slick version of the new 'Master Race' – and coming from a self-proclaimed, reformer and unifying candidate at that.

OBAMA: NO AFRICAN-AMERICAN HE

Barack Hussein Obama is not a descendant of enslaved Africans brought to America. His Arab ancestors in Kenya were slave owners and slave traders. He is half-white, a race which he largely rejects unless he is seeking money and votes, and, half black Arab [from Dr. Jack Wheeler, an intelligence expert].

PRIORITIES

Priorities must reflect what is good for the nation and the interests of the people. Record gas prices, a weak dollar, increased dependency on foreign oil sources, all reflect the callous policies and priorities of a radical-controlled, power-hungry, uncaring Democrat party, along with some faux Republicans, with few interregnums since the early 1970s. We have to put the economy – lower gas prices, avoiding the loss of jobs – and consider consumer interests ahead of rigid environmentalism. Tax cuts, especially marginal and corporate rates – because they create growth and jobs –should be cut, period. Tax increases eliminate jobs, because they hit consumers hard, who have less to spend, and spiral towards economic retreat, lost jobs, higher prices. A healthy percentage of business's profits are used for expansion, which results in more jobs, and more money in the hands of consumers, and so on.

Nobel Prize winner and economic guru Robert Mundell, in a recent article in The Wall Street Journal, said, "rescinding the Bush tax cuts would be devastating to the world economy." He continued, The big [economic] issue is what's happening to taxes. If Obama is elected, given his disdain for the Bush tax cuts, the U.S. will go into a big recession, a nosedive. Tax cuts are growth-spurring measures. Since Nixon foolishly took the U.S. off the postwar gold standard, the world has seen floating exchange rates that exaggerate currencies, particularly an overvalued Euro. Global currency rates must be fixed or stabilized. Now, exchange rates are driven not by trade [which they should be], but by capital accounts and movements, which are not in the best interest.

Senior economist Keith Marsden researched and wrote about growth in his work, "Big, Not Better?", published by the Center for Policy Studies. His conclusion, for America and other nations: "Where tax rates have fallen the most, exports and incomes have risen the most."

GIVING CREDIT

A President can advocate the following to help individuals, families, businesses, and the overall economy – if he/she can convince the Congress to go along:

* Lower tax rates for taxpayers, upper and other income levels, and businesses
* Reduce the marriage penalty
* Increase the child credit
* Reduce the 'death' tax
* Decrease capital gain and dividend taxes
* Enhance private sector job creation and expansion—taxpayers have to fund public jobs; private enterprise pays for private sector jobs.

If only a President and the Congress would follow suit. Well, surprise! Each and every one of those measures was promoted and delivered by President Bush. And each and every measure is currently under pressure by Democrats to be eliminated, reduced, expired, or overturned in the opposite way (e.g., increasing tax rates).

TAX CUTS

When is a tax cut not a tax cut? When a Democrat who at heart believes raising taxes is gospel, but describes the increases as cuts, and then goes back on his word and increases taxes left and right. Clinton did exactly that; so will Obama, if given the chance.

THE ECONOMY: GROWTH VS. HARMFUL CHOICES

Which states had the best growth rates in their economies and job creation, and which had the poorest? Former Sen. Phil Gramm and Consultant Mike Solon had a brilliant comparative piece in a recent Wall Street Journal issue.

In the 10 years ended 2006, the three 'winners' were Arizona, Florida, and Texas, with 2.7 million new jobs. The three poorest showings were Obama's Illinois; Ohio, and Michigan. Illinois gained 122,000 jobs; Ohio lost 62,900, and Michigan lost 318,000. The reasons for the difference: Governance, Taxes, Regulatory policies. In the latter three states per capital taxes were higher, state spending was higher, minimum wages were higher – each of which act to discourage investment and incentives towards creating new jobs. They make companies in those states less competitive, and that is what hurts.

Michigan alone lost over 80,000 auto manufacturing jobs; the Sun Belt states gained over 91,000 new auto manufacturing jobs. Obama's policies, particularly on taxes, would follow suit on Michigan's economic situation; McCain's plans would not. Will the nation go the way of a Michigan recession or get back on the Sun Belt track to economic and job gains?

THE VOTERS' CHOICE-I

What is more important to you personally? Making history (by voting for someone (primarily because he would be the first minority to be elected to the office), or making life better for you and those important to you? If you don't happen to vote for a particular woman running for office, that does not automatically make you a male chauvinist. If you don't happen to vote for a man who is on in years, that does not necessarily mean you age discriminate. And, if you do not vote for a candidate that happens to be part black, that does not mean you are a racist.

Imagine the following: Take all of McCain's experience, character, capabilities, and consider him to be an African-American; then take Obama's experience, character, capabilities, and imagine him to be white. Which man would you vote for under those circumstances?

THE VOTERS' CHOICE-II

On the topic of so-called racism, note that in modern times, North American and European nations are diverse, racially and religiously. Blacks live as citizens in these lands, Muslims, et. al., are also found across the board. But, focus on Africa and the Middle East and you find lots of racial and religious persecution and precious little in the way of civil liberties or rights. Some Asian nations aren't much better, and you can add tribal and caste discriminations to the list. In parts of Central and South America, blacks are further down the totem pole than those with more 'white' blood.

So when some politician in the U.S. raises the accusation of racism, and/or tries to exploit guilt or attempts intimidation, wake up to the truth! Particularly when that politician is black, in whole or in part, don't believe or vote for the lying you-know-what.

ROADSIDE SIGN IN L.A.

"A taxpayer voting for Obama is like a chicken voting for Colonel Sanders."

ECONOMICS FIRST GRADE

Dear Senator Obama: Reportedly you want wealth to be distributed more evenly. Should then the U.S. disown much of its wealth and give it to poorer nations? Incidentally, how would you accomplish that? How could you keep corruption out of the transfer and use? How would you keep equitability afterwards?   Apply your equality principle even more broadly: All families should have the same number of children – isn't that much the policy in China, aka Abortion Central, where infanticide is the rule? How about all sports teams mandated to play for ties instead of victories? Why not mandate that we all eat the same food proportions, drive the same cars, live in identical housing, and so forth?   Except for you pandering politicians and cronies, of course. Senator, you are either an idiot or a liar – or both! Your ambition is most substantive, your knowledge, principles and capabilities sorely lacking.

ECONOMIC WOES: BLAME THE PRESIDENT?

The President proposes, he cannot force the Congress to accept it. The Congress disposes, and the economy enjoys or suffers the consequences. Congress controls the purse –budget, taxes, entitlement programs, et. al. The Federal Reserve controls interest rates. The House of Representatives has the sole responsibility for originating and approving appropriations and taxes.

So, if the tax code is unfair, if the budget is in the red, if there is spending for the military and intelligence in time of war and conflict, the responsibility belongs to the House, not to the President.

The President does set a tone, policy, initiatives, makes nominations (subject to Congressional approval), serves as commander-in-chief (subject to Supreme Court hindsight), and so forth. The bottom line is that the Congress has more impact on the economy than the President. Even the veto power may be over-ruled by a sufficient Congressional majority.

Which brings us to 2006 through 2008. Before the Democrats took control over both houses of Congress, consumer confidence was high, gasoline prices were about $2.19 a gallon, unemployment was about 4.5%, and the Dow Jones Industrial Average was on its way to a record of over 14,000.

Since the takeover, i.e., the Democrat's idea of 'change', while Congress has fiddled with investigations, meddling, encroachment, accusations, obstruction, pushing for higher taxes, more spending and more entitlement programs, consumer confidence slowly sank into quicksand, gasoline soared to over $4 a gallon, unemployment rose to 5%, investment and home equity headed south to the tune of $12 trillion, foreclosures are rising, and the DJIA drifted down to around the 11,000 level. Of course, the President gets the blame for all this, even though the responsibility is that of the Congress. Also of course, the accusation that this has been a 'Do-Nothing' Congress is unfair – the Congress has been busy damaging the economy, holding up vital appointments, striving for co-Commander-in-Chief status while emboldening our enemies, obstructing needed reforms in energy and social security, and trying desperately to turn Iraq and Afghanistan into defeats, for political gain. Give them a rest: vote the darn liberals out of office!

MY FEAR

If the Liberals, chiefly Democrats, helped by a handful of Republicans, gain control of the White House and the Congress, I fear we will be inviting more 9-11s and other terrorist attacks, maybe worse; we will lose more of our liberties and rights; our economy will sink into a deep recession, taxes will rise left and right, disposable cash as well as home and stock equity will go down the drain.

FOLLOW THE YELLOWCAKE ROAD

No weapons of mass destruction? In mid-2008, 550 metric tons of yellowcake uranium were shipped out of Iraq and into Canada. The yellowcake was first discovered after the First Gulf War, when Saddam was left in power. Moving on, Khalid Sheikh Mohammed, the architect of the 9/11 terrorist attack on the U.S., admitted in 2007 that he was "directly in charge of managing the cell for the production of biological weapons, such as anthrax.

RACISM 2008

Today in the U.S., and as a matter of fact for some time, few 'white' politicians would dare be racists. But one cannot say the same for candidates that identify with the 'people of color' label, and, reverse racism favoring one race over another -- present Democrat candidate included. In his insolent 'Audacity' book, he actually stated that if things got ugly he would stand with the Muslims. The 2008 election is racially biased: 90+% of one voting bloc, African Americans, will vote strictly on the basis of race. For the record, I would have favored the candidacies of (the late) Dr. Jeane Kirkpatrick or Colin Powell, each of whom would have run on ability, experience, and issues, not veiled appeals based on gender or race.

Undeniably, racism and oppression by whites against African-Americans went on for generations. True, corrupt, thuggist white officials were elected and re-elected strictly because of race. Black victims and their descendants understandably bear resentment, anger, and, a desire to 'get even' by punishing 'Whitey'.

Even the otherwise admired and respected Oprah Winfrey, a first-line Obama supporter, refused to interview Gov. Palin, as Oprah thought it would be insulting to Obama. Years ago, Oprah refused to have Supreme Court Associate Justice Clarence Thomas –who happens to be black -- as a guest, because his conservative beliefs ran counter to the liberal code.

Nowadays, we have 'set-asides'/gerrymandering that guarantee specific minorities will be elected to Congress and state government – benefiting Latino-Americans and African Americans, primarily. Quotas, left-of-center and imbalanced Affirmative Action Programs, and current white guilt for the sins of whites generations ago compound matters. Another tragedy: the slightest negative criticism about African-Americans generates false charges of racism.

How bad is what could be termed reverse racism? O.J. Simpson could run for office today and receive a majority of the African-American vote!

MODERN QUIZ

Name at least three or four institutions that are not objective, not unbiased, not agenda-driven, not very patriotic, that also look down upon ordinary men and women; who are also contriving, corrupt, overbearing to the point of near tyranny, malicious, and inclined to favor special interests: Some candidates: the major media; Academia; most of Hollywood; and most Congressional Democrats, who are beholden to trial lawyers, environmental extremists, union leaders (not workers), the politically-correct minions, the educational lobby, and extreme gay activists. In contrast, the Republicans favor enterprise, and have a stronger sense of patriotism. Rescue America, by voting in Conservatives and voting out Liberals, top to bottom.

MEDIA INTEGRITY—ONE-UPPING HILLARY'S 'UNDER FIRE' MISSPEAK

Before Obama won the nomination, Martha Raddatz of ABC News covered John McCain's trip to Iraq. Raddatz asked 60 GIs who they planned to vote for in November. 54 said John McCain; 4 for Obama; 2 for Hillary. After a few moments about McCain's trip, ABC showed 5 GIs being asked how they were going to vote: The telecast: 3 Obama votes, 2 Clinton votes – no mention of the 54 who planned to vote for McCain! Sure, the media isn't biased…

ARTICULATE

Obama is very bright, articulate, almost messianic -- so was another, in that case, a far right politician promising vague change and accusing convenient scapegoats of causing his nation's problems with those attributes: a Nazi who led the world and his own nation to catastrophe. Which is not to suggest Obama is a Hitler, other than in speaking style and the ability to find scapegoats.   But, to be fair, an inexperienced and background-empty Obama is somewhat similar to another young, bright, stylish, promise-making candidate: John F. Kennedy. JFK got us mired in Vietnam, double-crossed the Cuban patriots, brought us to the verge of World War III, was oversexed, evasive and deceitful. Wake up to the real JFK – such as his true feelings about Martin Luther King, his inexperience, his insincerity -- by reading Reeves' book: President Kennedy.   JFK however, was not unpatriotic. Obama and his party scoundrels in Congress and on the bench, would strip our military and intelligence capabilities, appease dictators and enemies on request, abandon allies, and kneecap our economy.

McCain is an unpredictable maverick, but seems to be a man of honor with a sincere feeling towards the people and America. His judgment and positions on past issues as exemplified by McCain-Feingold, McCain-Kennedy, anti tax cuts, against drilling, immigration, et. al., made him suspect. He does have experience and background, he has 'crossed the aisle' for results sometimes constructive and sometimes costly. He is a fighter, not an appeaser; he has a mix of idealism and reality, and is definitely not naïve. He may not be the first choice of conservatives, but he could surprise many and turn out to be a darn good President.

HOW TO INFLUENCE PEOPLE WHILE LOSING JOBS

Promise them more jobs left and right, and fairer treatment, which are part of the Obama mantra, which, admittedly, makes many people feel good. But, the world and economics do not work that way. Raising taxes and wages, and, mandating higher benefits for businesses, lead to fewer workers hired in the first place, layoffs, and, higher prices to consumers. Raising the corporate tax rate makes U.S. companies less competitive than rivals in Europe, China, India, and elsewhere. It also encourages American companies to ship jobs overseas.

On the other hand, moving lower-end jobs overseas ultimately creates more higher-end jobs here to work on the final assembly and to add value to the product at hand.

HERE'S THE BEEF!

Americans have a legitimate beef over broad outsourcing – most of which has been done by giant corporations such as G.E. – to foreign climes, and, to poor 'insourcing' to areas of the country where some people aren't up to the job when it comes to consumer inquries and complaints. Language limitations, garble, 'mumbleitis', sub-par intelligence, unfamiliarity with products, services, customs and traditions, training by rote, and a host of other shortcomings are commonplace, and the frustration is maddening. What to do? Legislation is not the answer, because the only leverage consumers should have over suppliers is by the market itself, i.e., patronage. If you don't like the service, shift your business over to a competitor, or, don't buy in the first place unless you absolutely need to. Favor companies that insource customer service to places where the reps are up to snuff. Stay away from companies that have hired poorly educated personnel, minorities strictly because they are minorities, recent immigrants with poor knowledge of language and American customs, and others put in positions over their heads.

WHAT MAKES A CANDIDATE?

Fine, articulate, bright speakers from Ivy League Colleges, with law degrees? Hardly. Harry Truman arguably was one of the best modern presidents; he had a choppy speaking style, used plain words, had a limited formal education, was blunt and even given to profanity. Ronald Reagan was also damn good, he was from a small college, did not have a law degree, did have lots of executive experience, was able to communicate effectively, stressing principles and goals, not dreams. Neither Dwight Eisenhower, or George Washington, was a lawyer. Gerald Ford had a law degree, but at best was a mediocre, fumbling president who did not want the job and was ill suited for it. Jimmy Carter was a brilliant nuclear engineer, but so naïve he never met a terrorist he did not like. Furthermore, he actually believed that the

Communists would win out, and he could soften that by promoting his idea of human rights. He was the least accomplished and arguably the most ineffective of modern presidents, making one foreign policy mistake after another mistake and giving us double-digit inflation and interest rates. But as a speaker, he wasn't so bad – if you did not pay attention to what he was saying, instead of how well he said it.

As a matter of historical fact, lawyers have made for poor presidents, with few exceptions. At root they are exploitive and indifferent to what is good for people as a whole. Besides, there are all those lawyer jokes, and to think of one in the White House would be the supreme joke!

Incidentally, what do you call a lawyer with a double-digit IQ? Answer: A judge. What do you call a lawyer with a high IQ who is adept at deceit, disingenuousness, dissembling, parsing, cheating and conniving? Answer: A politician, typically a Democrat.

HONORABLE COMPROMISE

We may have different backgrounds, views, values, political affiliations, but basically most of us realize we are all part of one country: America. We are compatriots, and at the end of the day, which is often reached through bipartisanship and principled compromise, we should be overwhelmingly united in our pursuits. Most especially on foreign affairs, and, in times of war, we should stand as one. I hope you agree that those are the criteria that distinguish worthy candidates for the executive and legislative branches of government, candidates the people deserve.

POLITICAL ARITHMETIC AND ASSOCIATIONS

McCain would not be Bush Three. But Obama would be Carter Two, plus doses of McGovern, Dukakis, Sharpton, and Marx. As reported by Investors Business Daily, Obama's mentors include a militant, racist, Afrocentric, anti-American preacher; a U.S. black Muslim supremacist; an unrepentant terrorist; the openly corrupt Chicago political machine; a real estate swindler; and a parade of quasi-communists. Rev. Wright, Louis Farrakhan, Bill Ayers, Tony Rezko (recently convicted for corruption) and the lesser-known: Bernie Sanders, avowed Socialist; Frank Marshall Davis, a Communist subversive; Saul 'The Red' Alinsky, a radical Socialist; Gerald Kellman, Alinsky disciple; Nadhmi Aichi, a corrupt Iraqi exile billionaire. As detailed by The Wall Street Journal's John Fund, the Obama team continues to go to great lengths to cover up these associations and the attendant questionable dealings that benefited Obama.

Obama Sr., his father, was a member of the Kenyan Luo tribe that advocated communism. He wrote that private farming should be banned and that businesses owned by Europeans and Asians should be nationalized. Obama himself is on record as favoring a Global Poverty Act, paid for through American taxes, to give unconditionally to poor nations, especially in corrupt, strife-ridden Africa. Money solves few problems…

SECOND-CLASS WOMEN

According to a recent column by Economist Diana Furchtgott-Roth, Obama's plans would raise taxes on upper income Americans and worsen the marriage penalty on two-earner married couples (who would pay more taxes than if both earners were single). The penalty would be harshest on women who have invested the most in education, hoping to shatter the glass ceiling and compete on a more level playing field with men. Mothers would be especially hard hit, particularly if they seek the next promotion or pursuing upwardly-mobile careers. His claim about not raising taxes on people earning under $250,000 is a falsehood. The way his proposed plan works, persons now in the 28% bracket would experience a rate rise to 36%. He would also raise the ceiling on Social Security taxes and increase contributions to pay for broader health insurance, to particularly cover those that do not work.

IF IT SMELLS LIKE A TAX INCREASE

In a recent, brilliant Wall Street Journal OPINION piece in August by Kimberly Strassel about the Democrats' Stealth Liberalism, she analyzes the tax increases disguised by Obama as tax cuts, but in reality, are actually the steepest tax increases in history, a huge expansion of government, and income redistribution that will make taxpayers weep and non-taxpayers jump for joy.

His so-labeled refundable tax credits: a tax hike and income redistribution, falsely described as a tax cut for the middle class. Obama's universal health insurance plan: taxpayer funded government insurance that will ultimately kill off less expensive private insurance, owing to non-competitiveness and basic government inefficiency.

Obama's call for greater transparency and oversight would slap new rules on banks and mortgage providers that would raise rates and make mortgages more difficult and arduous to obtain by qualified buyers, and ease matters for unqualified buyers. Did you ever wait in a government unemployment line?

Did you ever lose a job to a less qualified person because of sex or gender?

He would micromanage the energy industries, rewarding wind and solar at taxpayer expense, punishing oil and nuclear in the bargain – which would mean higher prices and decreased supply. His idea of closing loopholes would result in a windfall profits tax that would result in higher prices and tighter supplies.

Obama is in thrall to Big Labor, aka protectionism, which opposes free trade, again with negative economic consequences. We had protectionism in the 1930s, and it led to the Great Depression.

All in all the Democrats are trying to wedge punitive liberal policies through the back door. This is change? This from the man that clung to his dear Reverend Wright until the political risk was obvious. This from a man that would create a Frankenstein, but tell us that it really is Prince Charming.

WAS IT....?

When Obama graciously spoke of Senator Clinton's withdrawal of her candidacy, was it real, was it Memorex, or was it because he desperately needs her supporters? By the way, Hillary Clinton, though she lacked executive experience, was more qualified than Obama as a presidential candidate, just by serving in the Senate longer and for having been exposed to goings-on in the White House and the Arkansas state house. She must be devastated, losing out to a rookie.

HOW COME?

How is it that so many of our enemy leaders, socialists, and others that clearly do not like America, openly and on record encourage our people to vote for Obama, and not for McCain or Republicans in general? The crop includes leaders from Hamas, Russia, Venezuela, North Korea, Cuba, Iran, and other 'nice' places. Duh!

DESTRUCTIVE POLITICS

Back-stabbing, frivolous investigations to make one party appear to be vigilant and the other look bad; parliamentary tricks; side-stepping the Constitution; spiteful obstructionism; making pawns of our military; persecuting our intelligence services, serve no useful purpose. In fact, they result in emboldening our enemies, handcuffing and compromising our defense resources, hurting our economy, putting our people at greater risk, and, making America look weak, confused, aimless, and foolish. Are you listening, Democrats and liberal Republicans?

DEFICIENCY

President Bush's Tax Cuts stimulated an economy out of recession, led to job creation and growth. The ensuing deficits, starting at over $400 billion in 2004, shrank each year thereafter such that by 2007 it was $200 million or lower, and less than 2% of GDP. The January, 2007 return of the Democrats to Congressional control of the purse reversed the trend, such that the deficit is rising again. Their stimulus and bailout packages are likely to result in a deficit of possibly $500 billion for 2008. Then again, an Obama administration that is devoted to tax increases, higher spending, and trade protectionism, will shoot it up higher, while tipping the economy into a full recession. If he has his way and a Democrat-controlled Congress responds in kind, the average take-home wages will be reduced by 40% or possibly more. That's change alright – but not for the better.

A TALE OF TWO LOCALES

With thanks to Georgi Porgi for a comparative summary, Katrina's impact on New Orleans and neighboring parts of Louisiana was a manipulative field day against Republicans for the Democrats, biased and inaccurate media, and other supportive minions. It was great theatre, given the poor black folks suffering in the Crescent City and its environs, and an opportunity to let the Mayor, Governor, local pols, and Clintonites off the hook.

Fast forward to flooding in nearly lily-white Iowa, 2008. Where were the Hollywood celebrities holding relief telethons? Where were the nasty, accusative Sean Penn, the Dixie Chicks, and their ilk? Where was the media asking tough questions? Where were the media reports of rape, murder, mayhem, cannibalism? Why did the media coverage taper off so quickly, instead of their daily Katrina polemic? Where were the FEMA trucks and trailers? Where were the relocation programs to free hotels in Chicago, Minneapolis, etc.? Where were the accusations that the Federal Government deliberately blew up the levees that failed in Des Moines? Where were the looters? Where was the wasteful spending of levee funds on casinos and other pet projects of the politicians? When did Governor Chet Culver say he wants to rebuild a 'vanilla' Iowa that God wants? Where were the accusations that George Bush hates white, rural people? Are the differences between the people of Iowa and the people of New Orleans that great?

THE FRUITS OF DISHONOR

What about loyalty to our sincere friends and allies, honoring our commitments, fulfilling our responsibilities? About 50 years ago, Democrat Presidents Kennedy and Johnson, and Republicans Nixon and Ford, made and tried, some mightily, to keep our commitment to the people of Southeast Asia. The media turned against the conflict, choosing editorial agendas over news reporting, the Democrat-controlled Congress withheld funding, and we were forced to evacuate.

An article in THE NEW YORK TIMES declared "Indochina Without Americans: For Most, a Better Life." What actually happened? As documented by Authur Herman, over 300,000 Vietnamese perished, through murder, starvation, disease and forced labor. 1,500,000 Cambodians were butchered or starved. Marxist-Leninist regimes emerged in half a dozen other countries, including Mozambique, Laos, Angola, Afghanistan, and Nicaragua. Soviet troops came back to Cuba, and, Cuban troops traveled freely to Africa to prop up Marxist regimes. That was the 'better life' for those left behind, and others, left to the mercy of the Communists. Once again, a partisan, biased, agenda-driven media conditioned the people and Democrats that Vietnam was a failed policy – despite the fact that North Vietnam and the Viet Cong were crushed and had signed a peace treaty recognizing the Republic of South Vietnam. Are there not parallels with the Iraq conflict today? Will a shameful chapter of history repeat itself, on a still grander and much more dangerous scale, owing to nuclear proliferation, and the global terrorist threat? Even more dangerous is the media's playing down of Iran and its growing nuclear capabilities, along with its belligerent policies toward Israel, America, and decadent European nations.

When does diplomacy work? Rarely, but when it is carried out from willful strength and the perception on the part of the 'bad guys' that the latter have a lot to lose and risk military consequences.

PROTECTING OUR FREEDOMS

We face enemies, nation-states, and terrorists, that so despise us and what we stand for, they would unleash any terror to cause us significant harm, while preparing to take control over much of the world. We have freedom of religion, freedom of speech, freedom of the press, freedom to assemble, and so many other vital freedoms and liberties. Our enemies would take these all away in a heartbeat – if they could – and they will keep trying. There is no persuading them otherwise. Force and the threat of force prevail. Remember, there is only one good Communist, one good Fascist, one good Religious fanatic.

THANK YOU, JIMMY CARTER

Take Iran, for example. Ever since Jimmy Carter turned his back on the Shah and let the mullahs seize power, capture Americans, set up a vicious theocracy, and kill, torture, and repress their own people, every single U.S. administration, Democrat and Republican, has tried diplomacy, incentives, all manner of measures – except military – to no avail. Iran has grown stronger and bolder, is well on its way to becoming a nuclear power, is proliferating that capability with Syria and Hezbollah in Lebanon, and who knows what other nation or group. Iran has broken promise after promise, reneged on deals, and thumbed its nose at The Great Satan and the rest of enlightened mankind. They have killed American troops in Iraq, provided weapons and material to terrorists there and their proxies in Syria and Lebanon. The West, including America, lets itself be intimidated and conned into letting it go on and on, proving diplomacy is the gift that never stops betraying.

Carter has also backed the Hamas terrorists, and back in 1979 he undercut the newly-elected prime minister of Zimbabwe (previously Rhodesia), favoring the brutal, murderous, anti-white, Marxist dictator Robert Mugabe – who is still around, running a poverty-stricken, country faring worse than North Korea (another Carter favorite).

<u>CARTER, BUSH & CASUALTIES</u>

In 1980, President Carter's 'peaceful' last year in office, there were 2,392 American military lives lost. In 2006, there were 1,858 American military lives lost, amid the conflicts in Iraq and Afghanistan.

<u>LIES OVER A BARREL</u>

There comes a time, long overdue, to be realistic about energy and its relation to the environment and even more importantly, the economy. Putting an excess profits tax on the oil companies would not lower the price of gasoline one cent, and, would probably reduce supplies. There are measures that would lead to lower prices, increase supply, make our national security less vulnerable to the whims and tyranny of oil producing nations, and, make for a sensible energy policy. The only things standing in the way of those measures are environmental extremists, liberal Democrats in Congress, trial lawyers, and environmental sympathizers – the mean greenies in judges' robes. Taxes, federal and state, are a prohibitive burden; reducing them would cut prices by about 50 cents a barrel. In fact, taxes are nearly four times the profit margins of the oil companies, gallon for gallon. In 1995 then-President Clinton vetoed legislation to permit drilling, in less than one percent of the land area, in Alaska, denying us over 10 billion barrels of oil that would be in the market, according to George Will. Environmental obstructionism, supported by liberals, has prevented drilling off our own shores. Tens of billions of gallons of oil lie under the Gulf, off Florida and Louisiana. Ironically, just 60 miles off the Florida coast, drilling is underway by China, with the help of Cuba. More oil and coal lie in the sands and shale in North America, just waiting to be developed. Ethanol, which is terrific for the agricultural interests, costs more to make than the energy it produces, and, mandates have increased the cost of food in the bad bargain. At about a present capability of approximately 4% of our energy needs, as well as at great expense and taxpayer subsidies, virtually all of the so-called alternative and exotic energy sources – excluding hydropower and geothermal, which are not feasible in most locales --pale before what we could do with proven coal and nuclear energy capabilities. Wind power and solar energy together provide less than 1% of electricity needs. The alternative dreams are either years away from reality, or offer minuscule benefit at greater expense; only their opportunistic backers seeking profit, false science prophets seeking funding, and the naïve are believers, the latter unwittingly falling for a great con job . We have been blocked by an unholy alliance from building a single new refinery for over 30 years! If we do not get on the right track soon, it will mean more dependence, higher prices, jobs lost, and recession.

A thorough examination of the political mischief and callousness may be found in "Gusher of Lies: The Dangerous Delusions of Energy Independence", by Robert Bryce.

No sizable economy can grow or even be sustained without carbon energy, from oil, coal, natural gas, and from nuclear energy. Politicians can talk about taxes, surtaxes, mandates, subsidies, global warming hot air, and research galore. Oil is the lifeblood of economic and societal activity, and, will remain so for at least a generation, probably longer.

Obama's and Gore's call for energy independence and reduction of greenhouse gases make pipe dreams look credible in comparison. Their motives are to attract attention, support, and votes or money, not to call for what is really in the best near- and long-term interests of the nation.

STRONG MAN

George Bush must be the strongest man in America. He has been crucified by the media, demonized and vilified by Academia and Hollywood for eight years, and he is still standing on his feet. Ever the gentleman, he rarely fights back.

I am convinced that if Bush personally captured bin Laden, and, cured cancer, the biased, ungrateful media would ask, "What took him so long?", and, "He spent too much money".

WIND BLOWING

Changing one's position for good reason, such as admitting to error, is quite different from being two-faced, such as saying one thing for political gain in the first place and saying the opposite to a different, opposing group, switching positions based on which way the political winds seem to be blowing. So are qualifications after-the-fact such as "Oh, I didn't really mean that!", parsing, twisting context, spinning, disingenuousness, et. al. – hallmarks of today's liberal politicians.

PANTS ON FIRE

Not getting caught in a lie is <u>NOT</u> the same as telling the truth. Trying to squirm out of an outright lie by claiming it was a 'misspeak', is a lie none-the-less. Not admitting an earlier lie compounds the matter when the truth is revealed.

THE DEMOCRATS ARE BETTER

Democrats are better than Republicans in many things: Lying, Corruption, Weakening Defense, Handcuffing Intelligence, Raising Taxes and Spending, Creating and Padding Entitlements to bring us to the shadow of bankruptcy for Social Security and other programs. Making a mockery of marriage, increasing Governmental power by taking it away from individuals, surrendering our sovereign freedoms to international organizations, playing the race card, being the lap dogs of special interests such as trial lawyers, environmental extremists, union leaders – but not working people, small business, entrepreneurs, and the majority of Americans.

WISHFUL THINKING

George Bush has done an outstanding job of fighting terrorism, even with one hand tied behind his back by liberals, lawyers, justices, civil liberties unions and their ilk. I only wish he was half as tough on Democrats, the Media, Congressional Corruption. Alas, too much the gentleman he…

AWUL

Absent while on unofficial leave. Barack Obama spent 143 working days in the Senate; he arrived, and then off he went to begin his campaign for the presidential nomination. His mark in the Senate is invisible, his accomplishments none. McCain spent 26 years in Congress and had 22 years of military service as an officer.

<u>AUDICITY V. PATRIOTISM</u>

The opposite of audacity is humility: Three of John McCain's sons have served or are serving in the military: Jimmy in Iraq's Anbar Province; Doug, a navy pilot; Jack, who is about to graduate from the US Naval Academy. In his book "Audacity of Hope", Obama wrote: "I will stand with the Muslims should the political winds shift in an ugly direction." He is not for America; he will not recite the Pledge of Allegiance; he rarely honors the American Flag. Maybe he should run for commander-in-chief of some Muslim country…

<u>GAY RIGHTS AND WRONGS</u>

Personally, I believe that homosexuals should not be discriminated against or persecuted for their 'lifestyle'. But, the court decisions promoting same-sex (gay) marriage make a mockery of the institution, nature, and Constitutional law. On the other hand, a good thing about recognizing gay marriage is that the couple will likely not have children – I hope! Another is that you don't have to worry about which is the 'man' and which the 'woman'. As for their divorcing, one can only speculate. The way the courts and radicals are going, who knows what will come next: Approving incest? Promoting Man-Boy sex? Sex with animals? Necrophilia? Whole new special interest groups for Democrats.

<u>LIBERALS IN BLACK ROBES</u>

The causes of declines, perversion, and confusion in many areas of American life – socially, militarily, decency, rest with the liberals on the Supreme Court, ruling on one thing after another that according to the Constitution, is not their responsibility or jurisdiction. The recent Boumediene v. Bush decision, as described by Andrew McBride, took matters of national security away from the Congress and the President, and undermined our ability to defend ourselves by waging war. Giving foreign-national terrorists the same legal rights as citizens, such as evidence chains, writs for habeas corpus, and extra-legal representation, was a devastating decision whose damaging consequences will be felt indefinitely. It also makes it easier for a terrorist to subsequently return to the battlefield to kill more Americans – which some terrorists have literally done. The alternatives are few: nominate and approve strict constructionists to the bench; pass new laws that offset suicidal decisions – or, ahem, stop taking terrorist prisoners... In my opinion, Mark Levin's "Men in Black" is a superb treatment of what the Supreme Court has become under Liberal majorities. Our nation needs justices and judges that adhere to the Consitution.

CREATING A CRISIS

From a WALL STREET JOURNAL editorial on June 21, 2008: "Encouraging moderate income families to buy $700,000 homes led to the sub-prime crisis." Bailing out the banks and other lending institutions that made such ridiculous loans, and who lowered mortgage insurance premiums, made it easy for people to borrow money to purchase homes they could not afford, and have put the housing situation in a deep hole. The same politicians who created the mortgage crisis, who curried favor with people to exploit their dreams, are asking taxpayers to foot $300 billion or more for the mistakes the pols and many financial institutions are responsible for.

What should be the bottom line of the Housing cum Financing crisis?

Should reckless lenders, investors and speculators be bailed out at taxpayer expense, or, should there be a genuine, sensible effort to come up with measures for only those deserving mortgage holders holding the bag?

The housing market bubble, which should never have risen in the first place, began with an overly generous Federal Reserve and 'class warfare' appeals in the 1990s. Greedy financial institutions made loans they never should have, the subprime portion largely became worthless, and mortgage-backed securities started to fall apart. Hmmm, which political party dominated the White House in the 1990s?...

POPULARITY AND POLLS

I personally doubt the reports of polls about popularity levels of the President and of the Congress, and the rush to pre-and post-election results. Firstly, the major media creates impressions of a President's so-called popularity, and in particular, through biased, negative, partisan reporting, attempts to obstruct policies and actions, and disenfranchise the voters. Secondly, there isn't any way possible, short of contacting a balanced majority of likely voters, to gauge popularity – and even that would be limited nor applicable for very long. As for the Congress, through coverage of individual Senators and Congresspersons, and Congressional leaders, there probably could be a short-term microcosm of sentiment

– but then again, members of Congress are primarily concerned with what their constituents think or made to believe, until and unless they decide to run for national office, which then becomes the big demagoguery play. As for the pollsters, any poll can be steered or manipulated into desired results. Polls rarely cover more than a few thousand persons, who possibly cannot represent the thinking of a majority of people. The polling group could be 'tilted' one way or another – for example, polling 60 Democrats, 20 Republicans, and 20 Independents, and then portraying the consolidated results without the breakdown, of what 100 people think, as the feelings of millions. In addition, there isn't any way to tell if a response is genuine – some executives I have personally known 'game' the system out of spite or to convey an opinion that they really do not believe in. I think it legitimate in a very limited fashion for poll results to be reported as being based on 500 senior citizens in New Jersey, 200 registered Democrats, 200 Republicans, and 100 Independents, on Tuesday the xth of such and such month, or the equivalent, is just that temporary result. To project that a survey of 500 imbalanced persons represents the thinking of most Americans is ludicrous. To believe those projections one has to be stupid, gullible, and without self-will.

I think it was in a Shakespearian play where some actor calls for 'killing all the lawyers'. Wow! Shakespeare was so ahead of his time. Alas, he forgot to include pollsters and biased media in such a sensible proposal. Well, not all, just so many, many of the troublemakers. On a similar view, President Abraham Lincoln said "Congressmen who willfully take actions during wartime that damage morale and undermine the military are saboteurs and should be arrested, quickly tried, and hanged!" Yes, he was a Republican, not a liberal, trying to hold a nation at war together.

CHEATERS' SURVEYS

The Wall Street Journal, in an early mid-2008 Cover Story, "When Voters Lie", revealed that people who are surveyed in private are less likely to lie than when an interviewer is listening. For example, when asked if they attended religious services most weeks, 56% said Yes to the interviewer, but only 25% said Yes in private to a computer. About 67% told the interviewer they gave money to charity regularly; 57% told that to the computer.

WHAT VAST, RIGHT WING CONSPIRACY?

Another big lie, promoted over and over again by Democrat politicians, augmented by malicious media, is the always handy scapegoat, the right wing conspiracy. Throughout the first six Bush years, the GOP, despite a paper majority in both houses of Congress, could not get its act together. Businesses contribute to both Democrats and Republicans. But the shoe belongs on the other foot: there is a tacit alliance among Democrats, Academia, the Media, Hollywood, Environmental Extremists, Trial Lawyers, and leftist judges, which is tantamount to an unlabeled left-wing cabal.

THE REAL BUSH RECORD

Up until 2007 when the Democrats took charge of Congress, Bush could be appreciated for, in no particular order: (a) A long run of economic growth, up from the 2000-2001 recession; (b) Tens of millions of jobs created; (c) Preventing additional 9/11s; (d) [To those to whom it matters] Having the most ethnically, racially, and gender neutral diverse cabinet in history; (d) Significant regime change in Iraq and Afghanistan that has saved hundreds of thousands of lives of Muslims and others; (e) Stepping up a real fight against global terrorism; (f) Reducing taxes to put more money in the hands of consumers and encouraging more capital investment by business; (f) Restoring decency to the Presidency. Little wonder that he has been demonized and vilified by Democrats and the major media.

LOOK IN THE MIRROR, INVESTIGATORS

Scandal is good, scandal is bad. It is good for Democrats, who love to put the screws to and to accuse Republicans. It is bad for the people of America. In re business ethics and conflicts of interest, in June, North Dakota Democrat Senator Conrad got preferential treatment and a discounted loan from Countrywide Financial, a company being investigated for loan scandals. His Democrat colleague, Connecticut Senator Dodd, also benefited from discounted loans not available to the average citizen, and got the 'VIP' treatment.

Dodd chairs the Banking Committee that governs Countrywide's market.

Countrywide was also especially generous to Fannie Mae officials Johnson and Raines—both high ranking Democrats that advised Senator Obama – whose number one customer is…Countrywide. Obama himself was the beneficiary of special, discounted treatment on two occasions –a below-average interest rate on a jumbo loan, no origination fee, no discount points to pay. The loan was for $1.32 million, for a $1.65 million mansion. The giant cherry on this Frappe is that Democrats are trying to get a taxpayer-paid bailout of mortgage borrowers and lenders, such as Countrywide, and, in the process, are holding up badly-needed reforms. Don't hold your breath folks, waiting for an investigation or reforms without a catch of some kind.

For the record, Senator McCain and four Democrat colleagues were involved in the 'Keating' S&L financial scandal about wrongful influence, back in 1989. McCain apologized, said it was one of his biggest mistakes, and he did not benefit particularly from largesse at the time. The Democrat Senators were less contrite then as now – what else is new?

SAVING PRIVATE (& PUBLIC) FANNIE AND FREDDIE

As reported by Lawrence Kudlow, it came as no surprise that Congress hurriedly put together a bailout package for government-sponsored housing lenders Fannie Mae and Freddie Mac, that will cost taxpayers hundreds of billions of dollars. Fannie and Freddie assist homebuyers, to the point of often financing homes that buyers could not afford to purchase. Their executives are compensated based on how much 'action' they reportedly, not actually, produce – a powerful incentive to pad. In turn, these same executives are huge contributors to the coffers of the same politicians that are supposed to oversee them. Millions of dollars flow from F&F to incumbent and powerful Democrat and Republican politicians, e.g., Speaker Pelosi, Barney Frank, Roy Blunt, et. al., and to so-called charitable foundations with a liberal or minority stripe. Former Fannie Mae CEO Franklin Raines, appointed by then-President Clinton, was forced to resign over accounting scandals –with a 'platinum parachute'—and he is now an advisor to none other than Senator Obama.

The Wall Street Journal described Dem. Rep. Barney Frank as the Patron Saint of Fannie Mae. Over just the past 8 years, Frank has fought off reform, dismissed concerns as to the financial health of the institution, stated that Fannie and Freddie posed no threat to the U.S. Treasury and to taxpayers, pushed both institutions into guaranteeing more mortgages, pressured regulators to ease up on Fannie and Freddie, even after the housing crisis was underway. He also pushed through a provision that mandates a chunk of Fannie and Freddie profits be put in a trust fund that politicians can use to disburse monies to their own special interests. Barney Rubbish would be more apt.

IMMIGRATION

There are arguments on both sides of the issue. Those against open borders and for enforcing immigration laws; those for open borders and virtually no enforcement. A look at some of the salient facts:

- It is a genuine national security issue, especially in the age of terrorism.
- Crime rates of illegal immigrants are well above average.
- The sheer costs of social services is mountainous and climbing.

- We are becoming a nation with an eroding official language and a rising unofficial second language – among people here that do not care to learn English -- by fiat, not choice.
- It is grossly unfair to legal immigrants that are on the right path towards becoming citizens, and, makes a mockery of the system.
- An estimated 12 million illegal immigrants -- I personally have no idea as to how they are counted, and believe it is an estimate that the media made 'legitimate' -- are now in America, and their population increases daily.
- State governments spend about $22 billion a year on welfare.

On the other side of the ledger;

- Illegal aliens add to the unskilled labor force.
- There are some jobs that many Americans do not want, and seasonal jobs, that aliens fill.
- There are humane reasons.
- They are a price-lowering mechanism in the economy.

Compromise is possible. Apart from temporary 'guest passes', why not let those employers who benefit from the low wages of illegal immigrants, and, those liberals that insist on open borders, adhere to an "Adopt an Illegal Alien" doctrine, such they, not taxpayers, are directly responsible for the economic, educational, and social impact of the illegals?

PS: Read "The Dark Side of Illegal Immigration" (www.diggersrealm.com) which puts the total cost at over $330 billion a year.

PPS: From Michelle Malkin: The terrorists behind the first World Trade Center attack were illegal aliens. The 9/11 hijackers had short-term visas – more easily obtained than a false I.D. underage youths use to get drinks in bars or to gamble in casinos.

PPPS: There was a sensible, bipartisan effort to streamline the application process for migrant farmhand guest workers in May, but, it was torpedoed by NJ Senator Menendez, a Democrat, who said that as a start, it did not go far enough to help illegal immigrants. He just doesn't believe that a journey starts with one step…

DID YOU HEAR THAT…?

In the event Hollywood plans a remake of "Snow White and The Seven Dwarfs", Michael Moore, Sean Penn, or Bill Maher, could be cast for the roles of Grumpy, Dopey, and Dopier; either Jane Fonda or Rosie O'Donnell could conceivably be cast as the Wicked Witch. O'Donnell, it is said, is also interested in the role of Grumpy. Many male actors would bend over backwards or jump at the chance to play Snow White. In the fairy tale, doesn't she marry a prince at the end?

COLOR ME DISAPPOINTED

As an ex-active liberal – back then it meant rooting for the underdog, combating injustice, promoting fairness, arguing for civil rights and women's rights – one of my keenest disappointments is the way former colonial nations, particularly in Africa, have evolved into tyrannical, murderous, warring, economic basket cases, driven by tribal conflict, corruption, and oppression.

You would have hoped and thought that they would benefit from the models of democratic, capitalist and even some socialist countries, and went on to establish enlightened societies.   I make no brief for colonialism; in these cases the devil is in what came next.   On one hand may be counted those nations which are even quasi-democratic.   Colonialism should have been ended years before, but as to playing the fool with foreign aid and relations, why bother, except for humanitarian aid that actually reaches the people in need, instead of the pockets of national leaders?

IT PAYS TO BE IGNORANT

A Florida teacher wrote about adult alien students in her school who receive PELL Grants – no pay back is required – to attend school. It is not unusual for the same aliens to receive free housing, free tuition, free books, and even a little pocket money. One student had a 'WAIT' card, used for free credit to get gas.

'CARIBE' is a special program – exclusively for non-citizens -- that pays for child care and other needs while the parent attends school or takes a training course. The latest request: The aliens want to sing the American National Anthem --in Spanish --or the anthem from their native homeland.

IMMIGRATION 101

There is no denying America was built by immigration – legal immigrants coming to these shores from Europe and elsewhere. Frankly, persons in servitude and slavery also did their share, and deserve recognition for that.

But, the modern illegal immigrant is a law-breaker, who should not be rewarded. Illegal aliens are straining the economy, health and education resources, law enforcement resources, and, to some agree, are costing unskilled American workers jobs. Some kind of sensible compromise using vetted guest-worker 'passes' seems advisable...along with tough enforcement of immigration law.

With tongue-in-cheek, perhaps we can reduce two problems – illegal immigration and high unemployment – at once, by paying the willing unemployed to track down illegal immigrants.

'THEY' MAY BE BACK

Those wonderful folks from the Clinton administrations' foreign experts, who gave so much, have been advising Barack Obama. With credit to Ralph Peters, the Albrights, Christophers, et. al., who gave us the first World Trade Center bombing, Rwanda, Mogadishu, Khobar Towers, the attack on the U.S.S. Cole, bombings of our embassies, the massacres in the Yugoslavian breakup, vital technology transfer to the Red Chinese, empty verbal threats against Iran, promises but no deeds for Africa, missed opportunities to get Osama bin Laden, and other gems of the Clinton legacy. Over eight years of fighting terrorism with lawyers in court – instead of using military means -- they gave the emboldened terrorists ample time to plan and subsequently carry out the second World Trade Center bombing. Through nearly eight years of the Bush administration, in contrast, there has not been a single instance of a successful terrorist attack on our homeland, because Bush made it a priority and did not use lawyers to carry out the mission. What was that line from the Godfather?: a lawyer with a briefcase can steal more than a dozen men with guns; nowadays, they also let terrorists off the hook.

FOREIGN AID: IS THIS HOW WE BUY INFLUENCE?

Egypt, at the U.N., voted against us 79% of the time; Egypt receives $2 billion a year in foreign aid from America.

Jordan, at the U.N., voted against us 71% of the time; it receives $193 million in aid.

Pakistan voted against us 75% of the time; it receives $6.7 billion in aid.

India, our new ally, voted against us 81% of the time; it receives $144 million in aid.

Kuwait, grateful for our saving the country from being swallowed by Saddam's Iraq, only voted against us 67% of the time.

Saudi Arabia, whom we protect, voted against us 73% of the time.

Qatar, Morocco, the United Arab Emirates, Tunisia, Yemen, Algeria, Oman, Sudan, Libya, Lebanon, Syria, and Mauritania voted against us 67% to 87% of the time.

Do you get the feeling that Muslims in general don't like us very much, but welcome our handouts and military umbrella?

All this and other forms of foreign aid are paid for by American taxpayers. Evidently, money does talk – but not very well in Islamic countries. In return, we also get higher oil prices from the producing nations. All this exemplifies 'throwing good money to bad nations'. Enough!

John Bolton, former U.S. Ambassador to the United Nations, hit the nail on the head when he said that everybody who participates in the U.N. tries to advance their own interests. He opposes 'norming', which is based on an international consensus over sovereignty, rather than decision-making as a constitutional democracy. Even after 9/11, the U.N. has yet to agree on a definition of terrorism. The oil-for-food scandal is a tip of the endemic flaws in the entire U.N. system. There isn't any objective, outside auditing. The United Nations, founded to promote international peace and security, could/cannot get its act together for the Holocaust going on in Darfur, among a host of other failings, including stopping Saddam Hussein, and neutralizing the nuclear programs of Korea and Iran. It is ineffective, biased, corrupt, tyrannical. The organization spends a good deal of its time and budget defending human rights abusers or obstructing reform, as well as burnishing its own image. As Ambassador Bolton put it, "it is foolish to put lipstick on a caterpillar and call it a butterfly". We really should get out of the U.N. and then get the U.N. –as Harry Truman would put it – the hell out of the U.S.A.

MAKING SENSE

With thanks to Diane Garvey,, why not help draft a Constitution for Iraq? Why not give them ours? It has worked for over 200 years. That is, what is left of it.

An observer explained why a Courthouse in America cannot post the Ten Commandments: In a building full of lawyers, judges, politicians, it would be hypocritical to state 'Thou Shall Not Steal' or 'Thou Shall Not Lie'.

FROM A GRATEFUL, NATURALIZED CITIZEN FROM SOVIET RUSSIA

Imagine a business or government phone being answered with: 'Good Morning/Afternoon/Evening/Day; Welcome to the Unites States of America.

[then] Press '1' for English. Press '2' to disconnect until you learn to speak English. or simply, hang up. [Then again the caller would have to know enough English to carry out the second and third options.]

There was a legislative attempt to make English America's Official Language, in mid-June, 2007. Thirty-three Senators, nearly all Democrats, voted against the amendment to immigration Bill 1348, including then-Presidential candidates Clinton, Biden, Dodd, and... Obama.

A COMMENTARY ON APPEASEMENT, FROM GERMANY

Mathias Dapfner, CEO of Axel20Springer, made some hard, factual observations about appeasement, as excessively blind multiculturalists advocate suicidal political policy, all the while encouraged by many in the biased media:

- Millions of Jews, Poles, Russians and others, lost their lives to Nazi Germany, because England and France, and a hesitant America, believed diplomacy, negotiation and appeasement would hold off Hitler.

- Countless others died and suffered when the Soviet Union's Communism was appeased, leading to slavery for Eastern Europe, and a global threat.
- Nowadays suicide bombings and other evils are tolerated by an appeasement-minded Europe.
- In Germany, some in the government believe that creating an Official State Muslim Holiday will spare the nation from the wrath of fanatical Islamists. Reaching out, indeed.

Harken, Obama and kind, Appeasement never, ever works.

OBAMA'S CHOICE

Nation of Islam, or, America?

M & M

Obama staffers and spiritual advisors Jennifer Mason and Cynthia K. Miller owe their first allegiance to… Louis Farrakhan. Other prominent influences beside Farrakhan include the aforementioned racist Rev. Wright; the anti-white, Caucasian Father Michael Pfleger, an anti-American, anti-white ally of Farrakhan's; William Ayers, an unrepentant terrorist. With Obama's friends like these, America does not need more enemies.

RESOLVE

September, 2007: The Senate passes the Kyl-Lieberman resolution designating the Iranian Revolutionary Guard a terrorist organization. It passed overwhelmingly – but was opposed by Senator Obama.

SENSIBLE CHOICES & DECISIONS?

In this day of $4 a gallon of gas and still climbing, choose between drilling for the 10 billion gallons of oil in the Arctic National Wildlife Refuge (ANWR), and maybe making it inconvenient for caribou movement.   While you are at it, bear in mind that Presidents George H.W. Bush (he was supposed to be an oilman) and William J. Clinton signed Executive Orders putting virtually all of our outer continental shelf oil and gas reserves – which could supply our energy needs for generations -- off limits until 2013.

As for the risk of oil spills from drilling off shore, the mighty Katrina hurricane caused no significant damage from leaking oil. Natural oil seepage off the coast of California is negligible; even Santa Monica, which had a bad spill years ago, is now in favor of off-shore drilling.

ENVIRONMENTALISM PROTEST

Patrick Moore, a co-founder of Greenpeace, left the movement years ago, for cause. The roots of science education and objectivity had been replaced by political activism and environmental entrepreneurship. Greenpeace supported a world-wide ban on chlorine, despite the fact that chlorine eradicated water-borne diseases, in the process saving millions of lives.   Then came the campaign against chemicals per se, especially plastics – the same plastics artfully and safely used in hospital equipment, toys, shower curtains, car parts, and 1,001 other applications. In fact, without chemical science, we would be back in the pioneer days with regard to food, clothing, medicine, energy. The more recent campaign is against phthalates, a plasticizer proved to be absolutely safe for humans. More brittle substitutes do not last as long, break more easily. So it is across the board.

Environmental stewardship should be based on science, not political agendas created by lawyers, politicians, business exploiters, and, supported by a naïve public.

A fascinating account of what unbiased science knows, vs. politically-driven 'fear' environmentalism, may be found in Michael Crichton's "State of Fear", a fictional work laced full of facts.

THANKS A LOT, OPEC!

Thanks for gouging $700 billion a year out of our economy. And thanks for buying up huge chunks of our economy at distressed prices. Plain and simple: Oilmail.

MRS. ROBINSON

Michelle LaVaughn Robinson Obama, in her Princeton thesis, described herself as a separatist, opposed to integrationists. She is not for assimilation and she is on record as stating she will use all of her resources to benefit the black community first and foremost. Poor Whitey, given her as First Lady, can look forward to being assigned to second-class status. With a spin on the 'beautify Washington, D.C.' sentiment used in the case of Mrs. Lyndon Johnson, aka Lady Bird, Michelle may possibly uglify Washington. Admittedly, life is much tougher for an African-American than a Caucasian, especially if the latter comes from a wealthy background. But a look at Cindy McCain's life presents quite an admirable picture:

She graduated from Southern Cal and was a special needs teacher. She became involved with her father's beer distributing firm when he died, has since doubled its sales, and serves as Chairwoman. Her wealth is her own – she and the Senator have a pre-nuptial agreement. She has been involved in clearing land mines all over the world, and, providing water and food to people in lands ravaged by war and in developing countries. Asked by Mother Teresa, she saved the life of a dying Bangladesh who desperately needed medical care, and, then when health was restored, Mrs. McCain adopted the girl. Bridget, now a teenager, is the McCains' daughter.

The Family Foundation is dedicated to children's causes, and Mrs. McCain also is part of a charity for corrective surgery on children's faces.

After two major back surgeries she became addicted to pain killers – something she openly admits.

She is proud and grateful to be an American, and she is a shining example of what a wonderful woman is like.

POST-ABORTION DECISION

While in the Illinois Senate, Obama opposed legislation letting a newborn that survived an abortion continue to live. He apparently does not value human life very much.

A BRIEF HISTORY OF SOCIAL SECURITY

Georgi Porgi, a sort of pen name for a bright, politically astute woman in NY, has forwarded a brief history of Social Security – something we should keep in mind before solvency problems and inaction by Congress result in the Program going bankrupt and belly up less than a generation from now. Social Security is our largest government program, the single greatest expense item in the federal budget; Social Security and Medicare account for about 7% of the nation's Gross Domestic Product (GDP).

• Democrat President Franklin Delano Roosevelt signed Social Security into law in 1935. It is a social insurance program funded through payroll taxes under the Federal Insurance Contributions Act (FICA). FDR promised the Program would be completely voluntary and that participants would only have to pay 1% of their first $1,400 – which would be tax deductible -- of their annual income into the Program. The money would be placed in a trust fund that would only be used to fund retirement and other items, and not for anything in the general operating fund. Further, annuity payments to retirees would never be taxed as income.

• Renege! During the Democrat Lyndon Johnson's administration in the 1960s, the Democrat-controlled

Congress took the monies out of the trust fund and placed them into the general fund.

• The Democrats eliminated the income tax deduction for FICA with-holding.

• In the 1970s, during the Democrat Carter Administration, annuity payments were first given to 65-year old immigrants who had not paid into the System – unlike citizens who had been paying for years.

• In the early First (Democrat) Clinton Administration, with Vice President Al Gore casting a tie-breaking vote, the taxation of Social Security annuities began.

• During his terms in office, Republican George W. Bush tried in vain to get Social Security reform to resolve the coming funding shortfall. Democrats accused him of trying to wreck the system, even going so far as to create the impression Bush wanted to take the benefits away from seniors.

By way of comparison, Congress gave itself a 100% retirement program simply for serving a single term. Which political party should you trust to keep its word?

ISLAMOPHOBIA, AKA GLOBAL SUICIDE

Columnist Mark Steyn, wrongly accused by the Canadian Islamic Congress of Islamophobia, has been so falsely because of his reviews and comments, all of which are factually – but not politically – correct. A few samples follow.

Danish cartoonists, Italian writer Fallaci, French author Houellebecq, American author Ferrigno, among others, have been targeted by Islamists with death threats, violence, lawsuits and more, with the tacit approval of government units and other institutions, over the contradictions between Islam and the Western traditions of liberty and freedoms of speech, writing, expression, and stark truths.

Ferrigno, in a novel about an assassin, mentioned the following plot twists: America will be an Islamic Republic by 2040. There will be a break for Muslim prayers during the Super Bowl. Religious police will enforce Islamic norms. The USS Ronald Reagan will be renamed after Osama bin Laden. Females will not be allowed to be cheerleaders. Popular American radio and TV hosts will be replaced by imans.

Paper Lion

Turning from a novel to hard fact, the European Union Commissioner for Justice, Freedom and Security proposed newspapers exercise prudence on certain controversial subjects involving religions beginning with the letter "I". Incitement to Murder? In London, masked men marched through the streets with signs reading "Behead the Enemies of Islam", promising another 9/11 and another Holocaust. Earlier, British Muslims openly called for Salman Rushdie, a British subject, to be killed per a fatwa by Ayatolla Khomeini.

The Archbishop of Canterbury has expressed sympathy for devout Muslims, no matter what they say or do, and has even proposed separate recognition and rights laws for Muslims. To boot, polygamous Muslims (as is the case now in Canada) are receiving welfare payments for each of their wives. The British government announced it would be issuing Sharia-compliant Islamic bonds. In the UK, a poll of young Muslims revealed that those that convert to another religion should be put to death. British Muslim nurses refuse to comply with hygiene procedures on the grounds that scrubbing requires them to, un-Islam like, bare their arms.

Muslim honor killings have taken place in Iraq, Pakistan, Yemen, Iran, Germany, the Netherlands, Toronto and Dallas; nightclubs, trains and buses have been blown up.

Dr. Mohamed Elmasry announced on Canadian television that he approves of the murder of all Israeli civilians over the age of 18.

In Amsterdam, Muslim fanatics have been attacking homosexuals.

Harvard University has introduced gender-segregated swimming and gym sessions at the behest of the Harvard Islamic Society.

A Swedish cabinet minister said we should be nice to Muslims now, so that when they are in the majority, they will be nice to us.

The late journalist Tony Snow reported that CNN has refrained from calling bin Laden a terrorist. He also said ABC News President David Westin, an attorney, ordered his charges not to wear flag pins because doing so would constitute taking sides in the war against terror. He also said to journalism students that objectivity standards forbade his rendering judgment on the propriety of flying an occupied jet into the Pentagon. If this tide is not quickly and decisively turned, Western culture and life will perish from suicide, courtesy of modern day apologists, appeasers, traitors, and their ilk.

HEALTH CARE PLAN

Obama's plan, which is more than ten-times more sweeping than McCain's, would cost about $1.6 trillion over 10 years, according to the Economic Policy Institute. Costs to be picked up by taxpayers, either way.   Under Obama, medical professionals' liability exposure would shift from insurance shields and federal legislation to the opportunistic, sue-happy, whims of trial lawyers. According to Dr. Scott Gottlieb, Illinois law has taken its toll on clinics in Chicago (Obama's home town), making it harder for some bare-bones clinics to offer [the poor] any services at all. An Obama bill required local clinics to provide specialized services, such as obstetrics and dental care, and special occupation-related health services for migratory and seasonal agricultural workers. Prescriptive mandates on covered services have proven to be a hindrance to community health clinics – especially given the Democrats' penchant for 'fairness' over reform and efficiency.

CODDLING TERRORIST PRISONERS

Oh how those poor terrorists are suffering at the Guantanamo detention facility. Barracks style housing, language classes, movies, better (Halal dietary) food than our military in the field gets, recreational facilities, climate control, mail; prayer books, rugs and services 5-times a day; access to telephones, restorative surgery, and more. Look for the Hollywood Left to make a film about their so-called mistreatment at the hands of cruel Americans. Of course, a film about Islamic terrorist cruelty – lopping off heads, beating captives to death, suicide bombing men, women and children, and such – would not interest those wonderful folks in film land. I mean, what group could hold a candle to the moral values in Hollywood?

To liberal Democrats, the legal rights of terrorists, even known killers, should be on a par with the Constitutional rights of U.S. citizens – and worse, the Supreme Court agreed!

BULLETS AND BOOKS

Our defense budget is approximately $520 billion, of which a minor share goes for the conflicts in Afghanistan and Iraq. Our spending on education is about $1 trillion – and school performance keeps sliding downhill. But since the teachers' unions have much more clout than defense contractors, it is as understandable as 2+2= approximately 4 depending on politically correct requirements, right?

VOTE FOR...

Vote for retreat and dishonor, higher taxes, fewer jobs, more terrorist attacks, more government running your life. Vote for Democrats!

CANDIDATE COMPARISON

One candidate offers inexperience, naivete', no knowledge of economics, good speaking abilities, and three years of community organizer work – bringing pressure on public officials to increase entitlements and services for the poor. Al Sharpton, who has been doing this sort of thing longer, is better at those things – but he cannot put on the 'act' Obama does.

MENDACIOUS (UNTRUTHFUL) DEMS

If the Democrats were sincere about tax cuts they would have passed the cuts or made the Bush cuts permanent by now. But they really favor higher taxes and more government, and, would rather not see the people prosper, because the mess can be blamed on Bush and enhances their chances of victory.

TAX COMPARISON

(Approximate)Income Taxes under Clinton and Bush compared:

Bracket	Clinton	Bush	Savings
Single, $30K	$8,400	$4,500	$3,900
Single, $50K	14,000	12,500	1,500
Single, $75K	23,250	18,750	4,500
Married, $60K	16,800	8,400	8,400
Married, $75K	21,000	18,750	2,250
Married, $125K	38,750	31,250	7,500

And Obama wants to raise taxes above the Clinton levels!

TAX FACTS

The wealthiest 50% of the population pays over 97% of all income taxes; the bottom 50% about 3%. Under Clinton, the 'rich' paid less taxes than under Bush. Under Carter, the 'rich' paid even less of a percentage. Obama wants to <u>raise</u> taxes, particularly on the rich, back to the Carter levels. But, by rich, he means most of the 50% of the population that now foots the income tax bills.

SEX SCANDALS: FAIR PLAY

Congressman Gerry Studds, Democrat of Massachusetts, in 1983 was censored for engaging in sexual relationships with minors, particularly 17-year old Congressional Pages. His colleagues applauded him.

Congressman Barney Frank, Democrat of Massachusetts since 1980, in 1990, was reprimanded for hiring a male prostitute who used Frank's apartment to run an escort service. Frank has been re-elected again and again and chairs the House Financial Services Committee. Congressman Mark Foley, Republican of Florida, elected 1994, resigned from the Congress in September, 2006, shortly before the national elections. Foley was accused of sending suggestive emails and sexually explicit instant messages to teen-age boys. Massive Front Page articles and TV News leads about the incident are believed to have contributed to the Democrats recapturing control of the House of Representatives from the 'sinful Republicans', after a long hiatus.

Governor Jim McGreevey, Democrat of New Jersey, married and the father of one child, admitted he had gay affairs and that he appointed an unqualified male lover to an important security position in the state. He resigned, but was lauded for 'coming out of the closet'.

Senator Larry Craig, Republican of Idaho, admitted to tapping his foot in a men's room in an apparent pickup attempt. His indiscretion was more broadly covered by the media than those of the Democrats; efforts were made to get him to resign or not run for office again.

Governor Elliott Spitzer, Democrat of New York, a family man, resigned when it was discovered he regularly had liaisons with expensive prostitutes. His treatment by the press was more a case of his truculent personality than of his 'sin'.

Former North Carolina Senator, vice presidential nominee and presidential candidate John Edwards, Democrat, owned up to an affair while his wife was terminally ill with cancer, when tabloid journalists discovered his indiscretion.

He admitted bad judgment, while ignoring reports he was the father of a love child with the woman, who was on his candidate payroll in a no-show job. Some Democrats suggested it was all his wife's fault.

Moral #1: Computer sex is evidently the equivalent of sex with a minor and of engaging a male prostitute on one's (ahem) staff.

Moral #2: If you are a Massachusetts Congressperson inclined towards gay sexual activities, or a Governor from New Jersey that was secretly gay, you had better be a Democrat if you don't want to be driven from office.

Moral #3: If you are a Republican, don't even get caught reading a porn magazine – unless you want to be a Page One or 6:00 News story subject for an extended period of time.

CREDIBILITY CHASM

Former President Bill Clinton claimed to be obsessed with the capture or killing of top Terrorist Osama bin Laden. He said that in a "comprehensive systematic way to protect the country against terror", he worked hard to try and kill him [Osama]." Yet, in his 1,008-page biography, Clinton makes only one mention of bin Laden, well after 900 pages.

A much more credible summary of Clinton's failures to combat global terror may be found in Richard Miniter's "Losing Bin Laden". Another must-read is Gerry Posner's "Why America Slept", which documents the Clinton's White House's goings-on, ineptitude, inaction, and putting public relations ahead of the public interest, which resulted in the unleashing of global terror.

TAXING THE RICH

According to author David Kay Johnston, Bill Clinton reduced the taxes of the super-rich nearly twice as much as George Bush. Are you listening media, lying Democrats, and voters?

READ MY LIPS?

George H.W. Bush promised not to raise taxes, using the phrase, "Read My Lips." But he broke his word and did raise taxes.

Bill Clinton the candidate promised to ease the tax burden of the middle class. In his first administration he raised taxes by $250 billion, especially hitting the middle-class hard.

George W. Bush promised to cut taxes, to promote growth and get the nation out of the recession. He kept his word, without any mention of lip reading.

Barack Obama is another canny Democrat. He has already pledged to raise taxes in nearly every nook and cranny, but he disguises this policy by calling it cutting taxes.

After opposing tax cuts years before, John McCain has now promised to sustain the Bush tax cuts, and his word is his honor.

ENGLISH WRITTEN HERE

I am particularly amused by all those ads about Learning English. How will prospects that do not read English understand the message?

IT WAS NOT FOR OIL

With thanks to Douglas J. Feith, former Under Secretary of Defense: We had many sensible reasons for going to war with Iraq; Saddam Hussein had developed and used weapons of mass destruction, as exemplified by his employing chemical and biological weapons in wars against Iran and later Kuwait. Saddam had programs to produce stockpiles of WMD and, was developing nuclear capabilities – perhaps with an assist from North Korea or Pakistan -- was next on his list. He had a record of supplying funds and other resources to terrorist organizations – training, safe haven, political support – and there was genuine concern he would ultimately furnish WMD to a terrorist organization.

After 9/11, America had a lower tolerance for the dangers posed by terrorists and their nation-state supporters. Saddam grew bolder and more ambitious in the face of ineffective sanctions; indeed, the oil-for-food UN program was a corrupt farce that strengthened his hand. A dozen years of working through the UN were impotent; the UN would not act to assure compliance nor did it have the guts to carry out its resolutions. Saddam forces regularly fired at U.S. and British planes enforcing the no-fly zones, which were aimed at protecting the Kurdish North and the Shiite South. Bush's strategy was not simply to retaliate for 9/ll, but to prevent another such attack. In light of protecting America's people and interests, since at the time we did not know with near-surety that he did not have WMD, we could not afford to stay our hand. The Congress, Democrats as well as Republicans, overwhelmingly supported going to war with Iraq—at the time, but for the Democrats, not very much since. Virtually to a man and a woman, they turned against the conflict, tried to hamstring our military, declared defeat and proposed we cut and run. More recently, as the tide has turned in Iraq, the Democrats are claiming it was their doing.

IRAQ, SI; AFGHANISTAN, SO-SO

The Iraq conflict was necessary for strategic and other reasons. Afghanistan has no strategic value; if Osama had not gone and established a haven for al Qaeda there, we would not have either.

FREE TRADE: NOT FOR OBAMA, NOT FOR AMERICA

Economic isolationism: undo trade agreements, promote protectionism, and see what happens. We tried that around 1930, and it contributed to a little problem called The Great Depression, marked by 25% unemployment! It took the nation more than a decade to recover, and led to World War II.

GLOBAL WARMING – THE COLD SHOULDER

Man-made global warming is infinitesimal, compared to natural warming. What's more, the latter is cyclical:

the earth gets warmer for some years, then colder, then warmer again. Note that scientists tell us that five times as many humans die from cold than from excessive heat. For the big story, read "A Cool Look at Global Warming", by Lord Nigel Lawson. To see how the global warming scam for what it is, try the "Politically Incorrect Guide to Global Warming and Environmentalism", by Chris Horner, courtesy of Human Events.

BIG BROTHER IS LISTENING, SO?

Electronic surveillance of terrorists, suspected terrorist connections, and 'bad guys': FDR, Truman, Carter, and Clinton – all Democrats – did it without warrants – not hardly on suspected terrorists but on political enemies instead. But only Republican Bush gets pilloried for eavesdropping on terrorists plotting against Americans.

PATRIOTISM, OBAMA STYLE

Let's see. Obama will not recite the Pledge of Allegiance. He refused to wear an American Flag in his lapel until he was literally forced to by advisors.

He had a quasi-Presidential Seal designed and struck for his lectern. He dropped the American Flag from the tail of his campaign airplane and replaced it with a symbol of himself. In Iraq, he chose to have a workout exercise after canceling a meeting with the troops. In Afghanistan, observed Capt. Jeffrey S. Porter, Obama twice ignored the ranks of soldiers lined up to meet him, passing up opportunities to talk with them or thank them for their service. Obama is on record as stating his willingness to meet without preconditions with any and all dictator-enemies of the U.S. – in Iran, N. Korea, Venezuela, Cuba, and so on down the line. But meet with a soldier – are you kidding?

TAXES, TAXES, TAXES

The good citizens of liberal New York State, reported Car & Travel Magazine, which is one of only eight states that impose state and local gasoline sales taxes in addition to federal and state excise taxes, pay nearly 70 cents per gallon in taxes: 18.4 cents excise tax for the Federal Highway Trust Fund; 8 cents state sales tax and another 8 cents for the state excise tax; 16.4 cents for state petroleum business tax; 0.5 cents for a state tax on petroleum testing; 0.3 cents state oil spill remediation. Then add about 16 cents more local sales tax and 1.5 cents for MTA transit operations. Thank goodness that as New York goes, so doesn't the nation.

And, Obama and friends want to raise gas taxes further, through a windfall profits tax that would be passed on to consumers, and via other means.

ONE MODEST CHEER FOR DIPLOMACY

Diplomacy can work if it is between two parties that respect each other, or, through a third party mediator whom both parties trust to be fair.

Otherwise diplomacy is at best a stalling tactic, and in due time it fails and costs nations blood, treasure, energy, time, reputation, and future grief. Likewise, sanctions are an ineffective tool of diplomats.

Dealing with enemies works through strength, aka meaningful intimidation, or pressure, impending threat, massive retaliation.   Take Islamic terrorism, if you will. What works: killing, capturing and keeping the enemy under wraps. Go further, and openly punish nations that support terrorism by one means or another – through funding, arms and munitions, training camps, safe havens, false passports, and all the rest.

In the event you weaken and think that is too harsh, remember The World Trade Center and other bombings in America – that our 'unbiased' media refuse to portray any more. Remember how joyous so much of the Arab world was at the time. Remember the beheadings, the torture, the slaughter of unarmed men, women, and children. Remember how terrorists will hide behind helpless civilians, or in sanctuaries such as churches. Remember the mass graves and the rape and torture chambers. Remember there is no honest reasoning with or satisfying an enemy sworn to kill you, particularly if he believes doing so will earn him a place in heaven. We would be smart to hurry his 'elevation', before he can do damage or even before he is trained.

INTERNATIONAL RELATIONS

Why worry needlessly about America being overtaken by Red China, or, for that matter, any other nation? What counts are economic and military might, and the will to use each asset. Diplomacy and political considerations are tertiary. Russia was supposed to bury us, Japan to eclipse us economically.

Those eventualities did not happen.

THE EXPERIENCE FACTOR

Candidate A, a celebrity, was elected to the Senate twice despite no prior legislative, or executive experience. Candidate B served in the House, the Senate, and as Vice President; earlier he worked as a newspaper reporter. Candidate C served two terms in the House and one term in the Senate; he had no executive experience. Candidate D has no executive experience and has served a half-term in the U.S. Senate. Candidates C and D have undeniable charisma and inspire people for different reasons. All four candidates have 'visions' for America. Which is likely to be more important for being elected President: the steady hand of experience or the hope inspiration provides? Vote McCain and Palin.

[Candidate A is Hillary Clinton; Candidate B Al Gore; Candidate C John F. Kennedy; Candidate D Barack Obama]

STEM CELL ISSUE: THE SILENCE OF THE MEDIA

Issue: Federal funding of embryonic stem cell research. As news executive William McGurn wrote, the position of President Bush was to support embryonic stem cell research, but not support the creation of life just to destroy it. As could be expected, liberal Democrats rejected that, and portrayed Bush as standing in the way of potential medical breakthroughs (in fact, he was opposing abortion just for the sake of generating embryos).

Not that the media covered it, but in late 2007 scientists discovered a means of reprogramming adult skin cells to act like embryonic stem cells -- translated, that meant there would be no need to destroy human life to obtain the cells. But why inform the people of progress if the credit would not go to a Democrat on one of their pet issues? Let's get some suffering personalities to belabor Bush and push for open stem cell research, right?

CLARIFYING ENERGY CONFUSION

As reported by Journalist William Tucker, global warming (by carbon emissions) and dependence on foreign energy sources may both be reduced by nuclear energy. Nuclear technology in the U.S. is so advanced there is virtually no chance of a reactor exploding, or of dangerous levels of radioactive debris, or of perilous waste problems. In the case of Soviet Chernobyl, there was not a sufficient containment structure around the nuclear vessel, nor safe operational standards.

Natural gas is considered the most environmentally benign of the fossil fuels, giving off little pollution and only about half the greenhouse gas of coal. But, due to lack of incentives and environmental rigidity, gas production in the U.S. has peaked, so the country has to import natural gas from Canada.

JUSTICE?

The Bush administration has drawn continuing criticism for trying to screen out a half-dozen candidates for U.S. Attorney. In contrast, in order to stop investigations underway that would have exposed corruption in Arkansas and elsewhere, Clinton had all standing U.S. Attorneys fired.

GOVERNMENT SPENDING

The Democrats believe in more and more government, more and more entitlement programs – to suck in votes while not mentioning who is going to pay for all those new programs or the expansion of extant programs. Portrayed as a carrot to naïve voters, in reality it is an octopus, with one arm in the wallet and one arm in the anus of the voter.

CLINTON VS OBAMA

The Clinton administrations accomplished some good during their eight years in office, principally due to the pressure exerted by Republicans once they took over the Congress. Clinton was smart enough to bend, and at the same time he tried to appropriate credit for welfare reform and other measures.

The rest of the time Clinton focused his energies on avoiding risk, wanting to look good, ducking problems, and taking little action. An Obama administration would increase risk, be tyrannical, create problems, take inimical action, appease the agendas of radicals, elitists, and the lazy.

DEMOCRAT MANTRA

Fairy tales can come true, if your lie cleverly, shift the blame to the innocent, stonewall, and do a good job of conning the people. If I may draw a parallel of sorts, quoting brilliant author Thomas Harris ("Silence of the Lambs", "Red Dragon", "Black Sunday", et. al.): A federal examiner (read ambitious politician, investigator, or bureaucrat) is someone who arrives at the battlefield after the battle is over, and, bayonets the wounded. What a template for most Democrats!

FOR THE BIRDS

In avian terms, Obama is a dove, Biden a pigeon, McCain an eagle, and when Palin spreads her wings she will soar higher than [the] Dem-birds.

THE GREEN MEANIES

Environmental extremists, through their political and judicial supporters, simply want to tell us a few things:
What to drive and what not to drive
What fuel to use and what fuel not to use
What foods we must eat and what foods we should not eat
How much energy we must use…or else!
Policing our thermostats
What kind of lights to use and how often we should flush
How much we should inflate our tires
How much we dare use air conditioning
Mandate trips to the recycling center
Mandate acceptable toilet tissue
Dictate what non-human creatures must be saved at any cost. and much, much more in a never-ending quest for control that could ultimately put us back in the Stone Age, and let some other adversary nation to just walk all over us and take over, when we unilaterally deplete our nuclear weapon arsenal, while the rest of the world arms up.

Environmental extremists ignore that humans are the single most endangered species among those species that count. Various political, not scientific, target proposals to substantially reduce carbon emissions will cost trillions and result in unprecedented job- and other economic loss. Limiting energy usage to that degree, according to environmental author Steven F. Hayward, would mean no refrigerators, no microwave ovens, no clothes dryers, and poor lighting, in homes, and, would also devastate the industrial, commercial, and transportation sectors. All of the so-called alternative energy schemes could not put current living standards back together again.

SWEET POSSIBILITY

Ethanol derived from sugar cane instead of corn is nearly 10-times greater in yield. But we don't use sugar because of the 'corn interests'.

GRASSLEY'S BLADE

For unknown reasons, Republican Senator Charles Grassley of Iowa, seems dead set against potential, experimental cancer cures, as exemplified by his attacks on drug companies and the basically conservative Food and Drug Administration. Some folks with terminal cancer, AIDs, Alzheimer's Disease, et. al., are dying to know why, reported Dr. Mark Thornton.

AFFIRMATIVE REACTION

With a nod to Gail Heriot, a Civil Rights Commissioner, there should be little argument against active efforts to recruit minorities, so long as credentials for admission or employment are not compromised.

DISQUALIFYING OBAMA; THE KENYAN CANDIDATE

Obama was not born to two U.S. citizen parents; his father was from Kenya. Reportedly, Federal law states that if only one parent is a U.S. citizen at the time of one's birth, that parent must have resided in the United States for a minimum of ten years, five of which must be after the age of 16. That means his mother should have been a minimum of $16 + 5 = 21$ years of age to make Obama a legal citizen. Since she gave birth to him at 18, he was not then eligible to become the president. She could have had him naturalized when he was 3 and she 21, but, naturalized citizens are not eligible to run for the presidency.

Even more telling, Philip Berg, a lawyer and Democrat, filed a lawsuit in Philadelphia Federal Court on the eve of the Democrats' Convention, on a number of points. Being adopted in Indonesia made Obama an Indonesian, even if he once was American. Berg also alleges Obama's birth certificate in Hawaii is a forgery, that in fact Obama was born in Kenya – but his birth was soon registered in Hawaii, but, strangely, in two different hospitals at once.

Berg also claims to have documents showing Obama registering at the Fransiskus Assissi School in Jarkata under the name 'Barry Soetoro' (the surname of his mother's second husband), a citizen of Indonesia. A recent article in WorldNet Daily made the same point.

Personally, I think that the obvious fact that he is not qualified to be a president outweighs the allegations questioning his citizenship.

FAMILY TREE

After the Pearl Harbor attack Stanley Dunham joined the US Army. Madelyn Lee Payne Dunham, his wife, worked in a Boeing plant in Wichita, Kansas. Their daughter, Stanley Ann Dunham, born in 1942, was to become the mother of Barack Obama. Ms. Dunham was intellectually gifted, did not accept societal norms, questioned authority, rejected Christianity. At the University of Hawaii she met Barack Hussein Obama, a graduate student from Kenya, in a Russian class. Barack Obama was supposedly born (see above) in Hawaii in 1961. Through his Kenyan father, Obama has seven half-brothers.

The Obamas were divorced in 1965, when Barack Sr. left for Harvard.

Two years later, Ms. Dunham married Lolo Soetoro, an Indonesian oil manager; they had a daughter, Maya. The young Obama asked to return to Hawaii for upper school rather than stay in Asia. At the age of 10 he returned to Honolulu, where he lived with his maternal grandparents. His mother, Ann, later returned to Hawaii and in 1992 she earned a Ph.D. in anthropology; her interests were in peasant enterprise, rural development, women's work and the poor – sort of pre-Community Organizer.

In 1994 she was diagnosed with ovarian cancer and uterine cancer. She died in 1995, at the age of 52. Her son Barack, busy with his first campaign for public office, chose not to be present, at her side at the time of her death. He wrote a memoir in 1995, "Dreams from My Father" – in which he states he learned more from his mother about his African heritage. Some gratitude…

SOWELLING IT UP-1

Thomas Sowell is a syndicated columnist known, among other admirable qualities, for voting for the person and not because some political party tells him whom to vote for. He wrote that Obama is a child of Illinois's well-known long and rich history of political corruption of the first magnitude.

He wrote that he has doubts about Obama's claim he never heard the anti-America ravings of Rev. Wright, pastor of Obama's church for 20 years. Obama and Wright also visited Khadafy in Libya, and, gave a lifetime achievement award to Louis Farrakhan. Obama's denials, as expressed by Sowell, were likened to a person attending dozens of Klan rallies and never once hearing the 'N' word. Sure, and Bill Clinton did not inhale or have sex with 'that woman'. Sowell concluded, "God forbid you [Obama] ever get near the Oval Office."

Sowell has described John McCain as "a flawed man, a bit old, a bit looney, with a notoriously bad temper – which perfectly qualifies him to lead us, in the face of the 'nut jobs' threatening nuclear Armageddon, blustering, rattling sabers, and otherwise running America down. I want all of these world leaders to lay awake at night and to break out in a cold sweat every time they think of messing with the United States of America," Sowell wrote.

[PS: Sowell is an African-American]

AS YE SOWELL- II

Sowell, a Senior Fellow at the Hoover Institute, described Obama as "arrogant, foolishly clever, and ultimately dangerous", not fit to be President when "the threat of international terrorists with nuclear weapons looms over 300 million Americans."

He wrote that Obama has a record and is in favor of protecting criminals, attacking business, increasing government spending, promoting a sense of envy and grievance, raising taxes on people who are productive and subsidizing those who are not. These scenarios are repeats of the 1960s: riots marked by violence and destruction were concentrated where the politicians were most liberal, promoting grievances and hamstringing the police – and not where there was the greatest injustice and poverty.

On foreign policy, Sowell likens Obama's views such as meeting with heads of state, with what was tried in the 1930s. "Those approaches, in the name of peace, led to the most catastrophic war in human history," but too many of today's young and those ignorant of history have heard about them, he concluded.

NEW AXIS OF EVIL

Author Arthur Herman put it very well when he described the new axis of evil as Russia, Iran, and Venezuela, all oil-rich dictatorships coveting what belongs to their more democratically inclined neighbors. Which is an excellent reason for standing up to the bullies with regards to Georgia, Iraq, and Columbia. Alas, I fear the Obama-led Democrats will abandon them, and as a consequence, the Axis will go on to more and more.

POOR BILL CLINTON

Bill (call him Casanova) Clinton's impoverished youth? His family owned car dealerships in Arkansas. That's just one lie in a chain of lies over a period of 40 years, says his Georgetown classmate, R. Emmett Tyrrell. Arguably, both Clintons may be considered to be the most thoroughly corrupt politicians of modern times. Note that if Obama loses in 2008, Hillary and Company will be back at it in 2012. Do you think she seriously wants Obama to win in 2008?

BEFORE GOD...

For some time I have images in my mind as to what would happen if Bill Clinton, Hillary Clinton, and Barack Obama had to look God in the face, and, be questioned about their honesty.

Bill is capable of looking God in the eye and lying to HIS face. Hillary would reply, "How dare you ask ME if I have ever lied?" Barack would say to God

"Only a racist would ask me a question like that."

PATRIOTISM?

You nearly have to put a gun to his head to get Obama to cheerfully wear an American flag in his lapel, recite the Pledge of Allegiance, sincerely have the American flag in the background. But he has the gall to put a Presidential Seal on his lectern, a Presidential insignia on the tail of his plane, and put a gym workout ahead of meeting with American troops risking their lives for their country.

THE BOO PARTY

The modern Democrat Party may be characterized as Bull-loney, Obstructionist, and Obstreperous –they are full of you-know-what, block needed legislation and decisions, and so ridiculously stubborn that they put the party ahead of the nation and the people. Example: $4/gallon gas – Pelosi and Reid refused to allow an up-and-down vote on drilling relief, and other prominent Democrats came up with one specious reason or accusation after another to duck the issue.

OBAMA CHARMED

Obama has enjoyed a charmed political career. The Chicago machine arranged for him to get the state Senate seat of Democrat Alice Palmer, an African-American woman that fell out of favor with the machine.

Obama ran in 2000 against Democrat Bobby Rush, for a seat in Congress, but lost to his fellow African-American.

Then came 2004, which pitted Obama against the favorite, Republican Jack Ryan. Shortly before the election the Chicago media suspiciously got hold of the sealed court records of Ryan's custody case, and published damaging material of a sexual nature. Ryan withdrew, and a last-minute substitute, Alan Keyes, an African American, ran in his place, and lost to Obama by a wide margin. The margin was unusually large, possibly due to the fact that Democrats still controlled Cook County, which in the past has tampered with election results – for example, JFK eking out a small, tainted victory against Nixon in 1960. Obama was now a member of the U.S.

Senate, poised to run for President probably before he started his new legislative job. It is well known that he has put more time and energy into his candidacy for President than he has performed actual work in the Senate.

There is not just a narrow belief that Obama's victories in the 2008 Democrat primaries were in part due to the party Powers' goal to finally dispose of the Clinton control, i.e., making Hillary pay for Bill's unwelcome, dominating presence. Hillary Clinton did win the popular vote in the primaries. This may be viewed as the wife paying for the sins of the husband, but don't be surprised that if Obama loses, Hillary will make a new bid in 2012 – unless the ambitious,

Machiavellian Speaker Nancy Pelosi, who is adamant about remaining the top woman in government, has her way.

LOVE OF COUNTRY

What a contrast! It is beyond doubt that Sen. McCain, who has risked and nearly lost his life, and, Gov. Palin, genuinely love America. As for the Obamas, Barack has been on a blame-America tack, and, his wife Michelle said she only first started to love her country when her husband secured the Democrats' nomination. Before then, the very unpatriotic Obamas harbored resentment and anger, and, probably, secretly still do. As for Biden, it is apparent he believes America has been a land of opportunity…for him…but has yet to show he loves America, as he claims.

NO ELITIST HE?

Barack Obama is not an elitist – just ask him yourself. It's just that in heart and mind he believes he is better than ordinary people – working folks, religious people, persons who happen to be white, men and women that serve in the armed forces – and he prefers the company of intellectuals, movie stars, the rich, the politically-connected, naïve students, and anti-American foreigners. He is the ONE to unite all the people?

BOTTOM LINES

Fundamentally and in conclusion, Barack Obama is a lying, incompetent phony and con artist who is nearly all ambition, of little substance, and a serious threat to America and its people. Couple him with both houses of Congress controlled by tyrannical, socialist Democrats, and you have a recipe for the disastrous decline of America.

If, by chance, should he, who puts 'black' interests ahead of the interests of all the people, win the election, do you think he will take the oath of office with his hand on the Koran?

WILL THE REAL OBAMA

PLEASE STAND UP?

1. No Certified Birth Certificate, No Baptism Record.

2. Claimed to be conceived in Selma, Alabama, site of historic civil rights march. Actually born, 1961. Selma March was in 1965.

3. Claimed Kenyan father was freedom-fighting goat herder.

Father actually was well educated, government employee, who war part of a corrupt and violent administration. Cousin Raila Odinga tried to overthrow democratic election in 2007 by violence, and create Muslim Sharia law theocracy. Killed Christians.

4. Father, who had 14 wives, was not a Christian.

5. Barack Hussein Obama is Arabic name, not Swahili.

6. Father was 94% Arabic and 6% African Negro.

7. Claimed he never practiced Islam. Actually registered in Muslim school in Indonesia; practiced that faith until wife Michelle suggested changing religion so as to run for office in Chicago.

8. Described Arabic call to prayer as one of the prettiest sounds on Earth, far better than the Lord's Prayer.

9. Claims strong experience in foreign affairs. Actually just visited foreign countries in Africa, Middle East and later in Europe. Lived in Indonesia.

10. In High School you were comfortable with the name 'Barry'.

11. Claimed to be a Professor of Law, expert on Constitutional Law. Actually just a senior lecturer.

12. Claimed credit for Ethics Bill – but did not write it, introduce it, change it, or create it.

13 Have yet to release state records (which show pork, earmarks).

14. Falsely claimed authorship of 26 bills, actually did author a single one.

15. Lie about opposing NAFTA in Ohio primary revealed by Canada.

16. Claimed to be tough on terrorism, but missed vote on Resolution.

17. Claimed did not take PAC money; actually accepted loads of it.

18. Claimed against lobbyists, but 47 have been working for you.

19. Voted against funding military every occasion.

20. Excellent Teleprompter Speaker; refused Town Hall debates.

21. Will rationalize or make excuses when caught in lies, or, pass onus on another rather than accept responsibility or blame.

PART II: PROFILING THE PRESIDENTS

The following summary portrays specific experience and other qualities <u>before</u> the individual came to the Presidency. It intentionally excludes such traits as communication skills, personality, charm, IQ, appearance, formal education details, popularity, and attitudes of the media. The summary does include whether there were allegations or suspicions of earlier, serious corruption. It also estimates whether each individual was likely to, or in fact did, place personal and political party ambitions, interests, and priorities, at key times, ahead of national interests.

The summary takes into account ranking factors published by historians, pollsters, researchers, psychologists, journalists, and others, based on the individual president's performance during his respective administration, as rated <u>after he left office.</u> These sources include the American Psychological Association's Annual Convention Report on the first 41 Presidents (in this study, all but Clinton); a 1999 C-Span survey of leadership, by historians; a June, 2005 Infoplease sampling of Surveys by the Federalist Society, studies by the Siena Research Institute, the Roper Center, and Zogby International.

PRES. & PARTY	EXEC. EXPER.	MILIT. EXPER.	AMBIT-ION RATING	CORRUP-TION FACTOR	PRIORITIES: NATION OR PERSONAL
TRUMAN (D)	YES	YES	LOW	NO	NATION'S
EISENHOWER (R)	YES	YES	LOW	NO	NATION'S
KENNEDY (D)	NO	YES	HIGH	NO	PERSONAL
JOHNSON (D)	YES	YES	HIGH	SOME	NATION'S
NIXON (R)	YES	YES	HIGH	SOME	BOTH
FORD (R)	YES	YES	LOW	NO	NATION'S
CARTER (D)	YES	YES	HIGH	NO	NATION'S
REAGAN (R)	YES	NO	HIGH	NO	NATION'S
BUSH I (R)	YES	YES	HIGH	NO	NATION'S
CLINTON (D)	YES	NO	HIGH	YES	PERSONAL
BUSH II (R)	YES	YES	HIGH	NO	NATION'S

N.B. – EXECUTIVE EXPERIENCE TYPIFIED BY PRIOR SERVICE AS VICE PRESIDENT, GOVERNOR, MILITARY OFFICER, UNION LEADER, BUSINESS EXECUTIVE. THE AMBITION FACTOR IS BASED ON A STRONG DETERMINATION TO SEEK THE PRESIDENCY. THE CORRUPTION CONSIDERATION IS BASED ON ACCUSATIONS, INVESTIGATIONS, AND REPUTATION. PRIORITIES REFLECT WHETHER NATIONAL INTERESTS WERE PLACED ABOVE PERSONAL AND POLITICAL INTERESTS, EVEN AT POLITICAL RISK; IT ALSO INCLUDES OCCASIONS WHEN THE PRESIDENT RESIGNED OR DECLINED TO SEEK RE-ELECTION TO SPARE THE NATION THE ORDEAL.

PART II CONTINUED:

BRILLIANCE AND BLUNDERS

Foreign Policy Under the Modern Presidents

Synopsis: A comparative, documented and penetrating review of the highlights and lowlights of modern administrations' conduct of foreign policy, from Harry S. Truman up to William J. Clinton, reveals the various brilliance and blunders of the respective presidents. * The main litmus is what each administration did in the face of foreign challenges and adversity, and opportunity, vis-à-vis in the form of other nations inimical to America or its interests, in war, and in the form of organized terrorism, and, with regard to allies. The many sources include presidential library material, testimony by administration insiders <u>after</u> the presidents left office, interviews, articles, books, and works by investigative journalists. Domestic policies and accomplishments are given just passing treatment, in the interest of brevity and the concentration on foreign policy and conduct.

Treatment, usually less than impartial as well as subjective, by the major media, and other considerations, add perspective to the comparisons. The emergence of television in the 1950s as the nation's primary source of information, as well as accompanying changes in major newspapers and national magazines, whether impartial, objective, and unbiased – or not – resulted in a more dominant journalistic influence on public opinion, policy, nominations and elections, the legislature and the judiciary.

The study is a basis from which to distinguish one administration from another, and, to rank how well or poorly each president served, compromised, risked, bungled, or even betrayed the national interests. The review reveals that some presidents would literally subjugate, at times, the nation's needs to their own personal or to political party priorities. As more and fresher information is available for the more recent presidents, they are treated more extensively in this article.

For perspective, the background, governmental- and military experience or lack thereof are included. For further perspective, the Democrats controlled both houses of Congress for 40-odd years, until the 1994 elections, usually to the disadvantage of Republican chief executives. That tide turned starting in 1995, and impacted Clinton's second term in office. At times, strong-minded Presidents were able to trump the Congress in certain matters, while at other times, the Congress did encroach on the Constitutional powers of Presidents.

Of the ten presidents—half of them Democrats, half Republican -- covered, in retrospect two were brilliant, most were average, three were unsuited or unprepared for the office, or, worse, and one was corrupt to the core. Each major political party had its share of exceptional, average, and disastrous chief executives. Only one of the ten went directly from a legislative position (Senator) to the White House. Five served as Vice Presidents; three were Governors of States; one was a career military officer. All but two of the ten had military experience which varied from desk work to actual combat.

To avoid great detail, only the Primary Sources are mentioned.

* The review does not include the administrations of George W. Bush, as (a) he is at the time of this writing currently in office, and (b) the criteria were based on information accessible at least five years after the respective individual Presidents left office.

Democrat Harry S. Truman: 1945-1953

A Vice President who succeeded to the Presidency after the death of President Franklin D. Roosevelt; later elected to a full term. Served in the military.

Harry S. Truman was an active, decisive president, vilified during his terms but later on he came to be regarded by historians as a 'great' president. His overall conduct of foreign policy was admirable, even in the face of a few blunders that would come to vex America. Overall, he came to be viewed as outspoken, direct, sincere, and a president who put what he saw as the nation's needs above his own popularity and ambition.

As s member of the National Guard Truman saw service in France during World War I. He brought about a quick end to World War II in 1946 by, after warning them, which they ignored, dropping two atomic bombs over Japan. That resulted in Japan's unconditional surrender; the dropping of the bombs came to be regarded by historians as avoiding the further loss of both Allied and Japanese lives.

Truman saw Soviet expansionism as a threat, and developed a policy of containment, and, at times, confrontation. Despite this he was accused of being 'soft on communism', particularly by a highly politicized Congress. He helped to nullify the Communist North Korean invasion of South Korea, promoted loyalty checks, signed the National Security Act which established the CIA, fashioned the Marshall Plan to 'save' Europe from communist domination. Truman ordered the Berlin airlift, and supported France in the early period of the Vietnam communist movement. Truman also encouraged a strong alliance with Great Britain, agreeing with Churchill's warnings about the USSR's expansionism ambition and its Iron Curtain threat.

Truman approved of the 1948 Nuremberg trials – and the subsequent punishment -- of prominent Nazis, which evolved, in mixed fashion, of how crimes against humanity would be dealt with. He also adopted a pro-Israel policy that led to the creation of that state and U.S. ally, despite widespread opposition.

Historians regard as a major blunder Truman's refusal to expand the Korean War into China and the use of atomic weapons towards that end. He fired General Douglas MacArthur for insubordination over those proposals, which contributed to the 'soft on communism' label and generations of enmity between Communist

China and the U.S. – aspects of which continue to create problems for America even today.

In retrospect, however, Truman saved West Berlin (and by extention all of Germany), Greece, and Korea from communist domination; he created the NATO alliance; launched the Marshall Plan aid program to rebuild Europe. Able to look towards the future and ever suspicious of Communist ambition and intentions, Truman supported the development of the Hydrogen Bomb – which was a high priority project of the Soviets in their design to dominate the world.

Ironically, in the succeeding Eisenhower era, Eisenhower, despite being adverse to the use of nuclear weapons, used the nuclear threat against China to bring about a cease fire of the Korean conflict. Truman was ridiculed and derided by the press, and the attendant so-called low-approval ratings stopped him from seeking a full second term as president. There were reports that Truman earlier had actually encouraged Eisenhower to run for the presidency as a Democrat, but, the latter was disinclined, as he felt more comfortable as a Republican.

Primary Sources: Truman Library and Museum; Alonzo Hamby of Ohio University; American History, 1877 – Present, by Mary Jane Capozzoli Ingui.

Republican Dwight David Eisenhower: 1953-60

A career military officer, retired, then elected to the Presidency.

The report card on the Eisenhower administrations' actions and inactions during two terms shows mixed results amid a good deal of vacillation and ambivalence over resisting communist expansion some of the time and abstention and reluctance on other occasions. A Supreme Commander, 'Ike' came into office towards the end of the Korean Conflict (technically not War in the sense that also would later be the case in Vietnam, since the U.S. did not try for victory over the Communist-backed enemies, but would instead settle for a 'tie').

After quietly threatening China with nuclear weapons (without an obstreperous U.N. to deal with), he approved of an arranged cease fire that left the North and South divided. [Incidentally, as of late 2008, a formal peace treaty has yet to be signed, and, North Korea's truculence as a nation with nuclear and missile capabilities is still a shadow over global stability.]

In 1953 however, the administration helped to overthrow Iran's pro-communist leader, Mossadegh, and assisted with the restoration of the Shah to the throne. Eisenhower also took steps to effect a regime change in Guatemala.

Reversing course, Eisenhower refused to aid the French in the Vietnam uprising, and settled for a North-South division that would ultimately lead to disaster. In 1956 he approved Secretary of State John Foster Dulles' opposition to the English-French-Israeli invasion of Suez. Dulles' reputation as a strong anti-communist was brought into question. Subsequently, as Egypt turned to the USSR as an ally, Dulles and Eisenhower realized the need for an ally in the region, and quietly nurtured the Truman-era seeds for what would become a lasting American-Israeli alliance. For reasons unclear, the Eisenhower administration failed to aid the Hungarian Revolution against communist rule, in 1956, which

Moscow took to mean it could continue to dominate Eastern Europe unchecked.

The administration was embarrassed over the U2 spy plane incident in 1960 – which may have been a factor in the indecision to respond to the Castro-led Cuban revolution. Eisenhower was quoted as following a policy of "restraint and non-intervention". Over the next half-century Cuba would be a troublesome thorn to the U.S., even bringing the world to the brink of a nuclear conflict.

The major media in America initially welcomed Castro as a liberator, but later on, upon his openly embracing communism and brutal treatment of regime opponents, the media turned against him and urged the Congress to follow suit. Decades later, a fickle and more liberal media would advocate 'peaceful' relations with and aid to Cuba, even going so far as to burnish dictator Castro's image. Cuba remains to this day a Communist state which abhors the United States.

Some footnotes in re Eisenhower: His basic belief was establishing a policy foundation that rested on the security interests of the United States. That translated into the protection of the people, accomplished through stability and security. He was on record as opposing the dropping of atomic bombs on Japan, and, admittedly, was not inclined to actually use the bomb.

The media then was at best lukewarm towards the 'reserved' Ike—whose style with the press seemed to confound the media -- over much of the two terms, and eventually labeled him as a 'do-little', consolidating president, anticipating a more vigorous, stylish and 'active' JFK. Moreover, the UN of the 1950s and

1960s was more pliable and a far cry from the UN of recent years; 'neutral'- and third-world nations had far less influence than they have recently enjoyed, which facilitated events.

Primary Sources: Eisenhower Library;Columbia University Library; Philip Kunhardt's "The Heroic Image"

Democrat John F. Kennedy, 1961 – 1963

U.S. Senator elected to the office. Served in Military.

Kennedy, or JFK as he is more frequently referred to, was and remains a popular media icon, but, who in the words of author Richard Reeves in his book, "President Kennedy" manipulated a willing media. Kennedy recognized television as the new and key medium for politics. He was charming, handsome, articulate, a symbol of vigor (that was opposite to his actual physical state as he had Addison's Disease), masterly deceitful, and held his image and his intended place in history well above the interests of the nation.

Spurred by the attack on Pearl Harbor, Lt. Kennedy gave up a Navy office job to attend the Naval Reserve Officers Training School, served as commander of a patrol torpedo boat in the Pacific, and was decorated for heroism after his boat was rammed. Major events during his presidency included the Cuban Bay of Pigs invasion, the Cuban Missile Crisis, the building of the Berlin Wall, and the early escalation of the Vietnam conflict – these were largely blunders and near catastrophes.

In the Spring of 1961, for political reasons, the JFK administration proclaimed that Vietnam was important to U.S. security, based on the claim that Vietnam was the prototype for the Communist strategy of so-called 'wars of liberation'. Some historians question that, in light of influential Cardinal Spellman's lobbying to protect the Roman Catholic minority in that country. The administration provided military, economic, and political support, expanding the conflict to the point where U.S. forces were directly fighting the Vietnamese enemy. That set the stage for JFK's successor, Lyndon Johnson, to further escalate the conflict.

Kennedy also sanctioned the overthrow of South Vietnam's President Diem in 1963, fearing Diem might negotiate a neutralist coalition government settlement. As described in LeFeber's "America, Russia and the Cold War", a neutralism solution was not acceptable to JFK. However, he hestitated to take firm steps to actually win the conflict, or, reach the point of a Korean-type truce which would leave the North and South separate and intact. This ambivalence was more evident in the Cuban Bay of Pigs Scandal in April, 1961, when Kennedy encouraged an invasion of Cuba by exiles, but denied promised air support and other resources for the mission, assuring its defeat. Also in 1961, Kennedy and Soviet Premier Khrushchev met in Vienna to discuss a range of issues, and to let each 'size up the other'. JFK concluded the meeting went badly for his status, and that would influence the rest of the conduct of his presidency for the balance of is term. In August of 1961 the communists erected the 'Berlin Wall', which prevented the free passage of people between East and West Berlin, and some speculate that the Soviet leadership concluded Kennedy was a weak, inexperienced leader who would do little about the Wall. American spy planes took photographs of a Soviet intermediate-range ballistic missile site under construction in Cuba, precipitating what became known as the Cuban Missile Crisis of 1962. If the American administration did nothing about this, it would lead to a perpetual threat of enemy nuclear weapons in close proximity. JFK also thought that if the U.S. attacked the site it may lead to nuclear war with the Soviets.

In typical Kennedy fashion he decided on a middle ground: a naval blockade of Cuba. To the public it was presented as the brink of nuclear war, but covertly, Kennedy and Khrushchev reached agreement: The U.S. promised never to invade Cuba, and, secretly agreed to remove its ballistic missiles in Turkey, in exchange for the Soviets' overt removal of their missiles. Kennedy did push for a Limited or Partial Test Ban Treaty that would limit testing strictly to underground sites. The U.S., Great Britain, and the Soviet Union were the initial signatories to the treaty, in 1963. Despite these precautions and intentions, the world would witness a proliferation of nuclear weapons that continues even today. Kennedy also sought to contain communism in Latin America by establishing the Alliance for Progress, which provided aid to troubled countries in the region and established a basis for greater human rights. The treaty enjoyed some limited success, but communist expansion attempts continued in Central and South America, no doubt inspired by the Cuban model. Despite all of JFK's blunders, the media, during and especially after his administration, bought into an image of the Camelot fairy tale – a brief, shining moment of a beneficent ruler – to portray JFK's promise and tenure – which persists to this day, despite the growing evidence of his deceits and disasters. He was assassinated in November, 1963.

Over time, historians and investigative reporters have been chipping away at his image, placing Kennedy on a lower rung of the presidential accomplishment ladder than the public and JFK insiders would have posterity accept. He remains a legend to most Democrats and liberals to this day, with little mention of his leading America into the Vietnam quagmire.

Primary Sources: John F. Kennedy Library; The Documentary History of the John F. Kennedy Presidency, Lewis Gould, Editor, University of Texas; The Dark Side of Camelot, Seymour Hersh; President Kennedy: Profile of Power, Richard Reeves; A Question of Character: A Life of John F. Kennedy, Thomas Reeves.

Democrat Lyndon B. Johnson: 1963-1968

Vice President who succeeded to office upon the death of President Kennedy. Won a full term on his own afterwards in a landslide. Served in the Military.

Johnson was more often known as LBJ and was sometimes referred to as 'Landslide Johnson' because he questionably won a Texas primary contest by 40-odd votes out of thousands cast. He was largely under a cloud, as covered by the media, during his tenure. He was suspected of complicity in the assassination of his predecessor, JFK; he was viewed as manipulative before and during his position as majority leader in the Senate;

he was looked askance at because he was a Texan and a Southerner in the midst of the civil rights struggles; and his main successes were considered by the biased major media – at times inaccurately and unfairly -- to be credited to JFK's programs and policies. But it was Johnson that got those measures through the Congress and implemented. On the downside, he received more of the blame for the Vietnam problems, despite inheriting what JFK had previously wrought.

Johnson volunteered to serve in the U.S. Navy almost immediately after Pearl Harbor, and was decorated for his activities in aerial combat in the Pacific. As JFK's Vice President, Johnson had a good deal of foreign exposure in missions to the Middle East, Europe, Latin America, Africa, Asia, and, Vietnam. Earlier and after he became President, Johnson was a major figure in America's Space Program, in large part because of competition with the Soviet Union.

In '64 he ordered air strikes against North Vietnam, and, it was said, contrived what was known as the Gulf of Tonkin Resolution as a rationale for escalating the Vietnam conflict. Reportedly, but unproven, his administration had drafted the resolution prior to the incidents of attacks of U.S. vessels by North Vietnam. During the Johnson administration, from 1963 forward, a considerable number of National Security Action Memoranda were issued, dealing with a wide range of foreign policy matters. They included many about Vietnam, which became a consuming issue, as well as nuclear energy and weapons, international-trade and -relations, NATO, and concern about the return of missiles to Cuba. Memoranda also covered aid to Indonesia, India, Pakistan, South Africa and other subjects vis-à-vis Israel, Libya, Cyprus, France, Panama, Latin America, Korea, Eastern Europe, and the USSR.

On the one hand, Johnson sought unity, particularly from other so-called allied nations, for supporting the Vietnam mission; on the other he claimed his main objectives were to promote peace and to build bridges to Eastern European countries. In what much later, though little known, would be viewed as ironic, upon deteriorating relations with Pakistan, LBJ provided military aid to Iran as a regional alternative. Hounded especially by the press over his management of the Vietnam conflict, Johnson, sensing his unpopularity, had the grace to announce he would not be a candidate for re-election to the presidency in 1968. A critical occurrence that year, was an editorial (not news) report by CBS Television News Anchor Walter Cronkite, considered to be the most trusted media figure in America, following the Tet Offensive in Vietnam. To this day, supported by fact, military experts and historians view the Tet Offensive as a costly failure for the Viet Cong.

But, Cronkite departed from objective reporting and added a personal commentary that the "war would end in a stalemate" – "nor could the U.S. win". This pushed the Democratic Congress further on to withholding funds, and along the path to withdrawal.

Military and other historians believed the combination of the media and Congress turning against the conflict also deteriorated support among the public. This turned what would have probably been a victory or acceptable end to hostilities, whereby two Vietnams could have co-existed.

Recently, and even more pronounced, television journalists and editors of major newspapers and magazines have similarly injected personal commentary and treatment, and agenda-driven coverage, into what are supposed to be objective and balanced reporting, on Iraq and Afghanistan, and other foreign matters (see Panel A) below.

In the cases of Democrat LBJ and his Republican successors in particular, that odious media practice has continued to impact foreign policy, split public opinion in the United States, compromise alliances and neutrality, and, embolden enemies and terrorists. With the passage of time since 1968, the LBJ administration as a subject seems to have faded in the media. The onus for the collapse in Vietnam was for the most part placed at the feet of his successor, Republican Richard Nixon, with the media unjustly assigning far less responsibility to either LBJ or JFK, moreso the former of the two.

Primary Sources: Lyndon B. Johnson Library and Museum; Summaries of History Professor Joe Franz, University of Texas; Articles by journalist Peter Braestrup.

PANEL A: THE PEOPLES RIGHT TO KNOW BECOMES THEIR MISFORTUNE TO BE MISINFORMED

The August, 2006 issue of IMPRIMUS carries a well-documented article by veteran Washington, DC Editor Fred Barnes: "Is the mainstream Media Fair and Balanced?" It artfully makes the case that major newspapers, wire services, broadcast- and cable-television stations, are intentionally biased, agenda-driven, malicious, and overwhelmingly liberal and pro-Democrats in coverage, at the expense of conservatives and Republicans, as well as balanced and accurate reporting. The New York Historical Society's Fall 2006/Winter 2007 program, "Politics and the Press in American History", speciously presented the claim that the role of the press has shifted dramatically, from openly advancing partisan politics to idealized objective reporting. A follow-up program addressed "Editorial Pages in a Time of Bitter Politics", and asked, in today's atmosphere of extreme partisanship, how do journalists manage to maintain objectivity during these divisive times? Brazenly, both programs' panelists are dominated by editors of THE NEW YORK TIMES, which is hardly a bastion of objectivity.

In the admittedly editorialized opinion of the author of this article, a more appropriate description for recent-vintage 'mainstream' media, should be the 'left-bank media'.

Republican Richard M. Nixon: 1969-1975

Narrowly elected to the Presidency on his second try for the Office, and re-elected in a landslide four years later. Resigned the Office in the middle of his second term. Served in the Military.

Arguably, no modern President, up to his day, was as vilified by the major media as Richard Nixon. He was also viewed negatively as a Congressman and then Senator, largely ignored as Vice President, treated unkindly twice: as an unsuccessful 1960 candidate for the Presidency and later on the unsuccessful candidate for Governor of California in 1962. He is noted for telling the press that it "would not have Richard Nixon to kick around any more". Some of these criticisms were the result of his own doing: wittingly or not, he created political and journalist enemies, and, his background, earlier record, and practices.

Nixon made a comeback in 1968 when he was elected President, but throughout his tenure his press coverage went from grudging acceptance to skepticism to hostility to his being demonized as evasive and a liar and a crook. Often referred to as "Tricky Dicky', he was nonetheless re-elected in 1972 by one of the largest landslides ever, running against a dovish, socialist-leaning Senator, George McGovern. Upon completing his service as a Navy Lieutenant Commander in the Pacific, he practiced law, ran for Congress, and was selected as Eisenhower's running mate. Given a range of major duties, Nixon visited over 50 foreign countries and temporarily filled in for Eisenhower during the latter's heart attack.

Foreign Policy was the top priority for Nixon; he had comparatively little interest in domestic matters and left those to his Cabinet and others (the domestic accomplishments included the end of the draft, a broad environmental program, tougher anticrime laws, revenue sharing, and triumph in space with Americans landing on the Moon, but then and afterwards, little recognition and credit was forthcoming.).

Nixon actually made an attempt to win the Vietnam conflict or at least force North Vietnam to seek a truce. But he was thwarted by the media and dovish Democrats, who accused him of escalating the conflict.

His stated strategic objective was the quest for world stability – and that was marked by reduced tensions with the USSR and China; a treaty limiting strategic nuclear weapons, and a flawed peace accord with North Vietnam. Nixon also negotiated disengagement agreements between Egypt and Syria, with Israel.

Nixon reportedly reversed a long-standing State Department policy of briefing the Soviets on the progress of talks with Red China, to reassure the Moscow regime. That sat well with Red China.

Nixon had his own approach to foreign policy. Rather than preside and decide, which was the common practice, Nixon also sought operational control, often in secret. He was skeptical of the 'liberal' State Department and accordingly gave much higher status to the National Security Council (NSC) and his top advisor, Henry Kissinger. While Nixon welcomed thorough analysis, he personally intended to take an active part in major initiatives that could reshape relationships among the major powers. In contrast to Eisenhower, Nixon little regard for decentralizing, delegation, or lower-level personnel. Traditionally, when a new administration comes in, the political appointees of the previous administration leave, and what remains are career people holdovers, who often do not have the same loyalty to a new administration's leadership and policies. Indeed, in Nixon's case, for example, few among the NSC staff he had inherited had voted for him. Daniel Ellsberg, a RAND corporation analyst involved in national security matters, smuggled the highly secret Pentagon Papers and leaked their publication by the New York Times and the Washington Post. That may have led to the "plumbers" episode (spying on the opposition Party) and to the broader Watergate scandal, which ultimately led to the impeachment process. Nixon resigned rather than see the nation torn apart by the prospect of an impeachment process.

Years after leaving office, Nixon received some grudging admiration for his foreign policy accomplishments.

Primary Sources: The Richard Nixon Library and Birthplace; Nixon Presidential Materials at the National Archives; The 1998 National Security Council Project, Daailder and Destler, Center for International and Security Studies, University of Maryland; and, the Brookings Institution.

Republican Gerald R. Ford: 1974 – 1977

Ford, a popular Congressman who replaced Spiro Agnew in 1973 as Nixon's Vice President, became President when Nixon resigned from the Office. Ford ran for a full term on his own in 1976, but was defeated by Jimmy Carter. Ford served in the military.

Many historians believe that Ford had no presidential ambitions, and, was even reluctant to run for election for a full term in 1976 – but did so as a party loyalist and to stave off a challenge by the Republican's conservative wing, led by Governor Ronald Reagan.

Throughout his tenure Ford suffered from lukewarm treatment and ridicule by the media, for a variety of reasons: he was considered to be an intellectual lightweight, his pratfalls and blunders (e.g., in a second presidential debate he stated "There was no Soviet domination over Eastern Europe".) received wide attention, he inherited resentment over the Nixon Watergate scandal and associated criminal allegations, and, later on, for pardoning Nixon.

Even earlier, he was ridiculed for co-hosting what was known as the 'Ev (Senator Everett Dirkson) and Jerry (Ford) Show', a GOP alternative 'voice' to the policies of then-president Lyndon Johnson. Ford, as a law student, joined an isolationist group determined to keep America out of World War II. That position changed months after the attack on Pearl Harbor: Ford received a commission as an Ensign in the Navy Reserve and applied for sea duty. His ship was very active in the Pacific Theatre, and Ford received many decorations. Ford returned to the U.S. as what he himself described as a converted internationalist, and he went on to a long and popular career in the House of Representatives.

As Vice President Ford was largely ignored by the major media; as President he received little attention, save for the occasional gaffe – but primarily because of the incessant post-coverage of Watergate and the attendant voter dissatisfaction. When Congress withdrew funding for the Vietnam Conflict, the Ford administration had no alternative but to oversee the final withdrawal of U.S. personnel from Vietnam, in April, 1975. North Vietnam invaded the South, and the Indochina bloodbath began. In addition to inheriting the Vietnam situation, Ford also inherited the discussions about detente with Russia and of building ties with Communist China.

In 1975 Ford signed the Helsinki Accords with the Soviet Union, a framework to monitor compliance with Strategic Arms Limitations. Two other incidents marked his tenure in the White House: the seizure of the American merchant ship Mayaguez by Cambodia, which led to U.S. casualties, and, negotiations to cede the Panama Canal.

In broad retrospect, the withdrawal from Vietnam, the collapse of other Indochina nations, the disunity in America, doubts about both the USSR and Red China, all contributed to a perception of U.S. weakness that emboldened its adversaries. Many thought Ford was essentially a fill-in without ambition or initiative, not worthy of the usual respect given an ex- President, an essentially unremarkable 'nice guy' who left office without a meaningful legacy. Many years later Ford received some credit for restoring decency to the White House. But, historians believe Ford bore the brunt of the blame for Nixon's perceived 'sins'.

Primary Sources: American Presidents, History: Gerald R. Ford; Gerald R. Ford Presidential Library and Museum; J.R. Greene, The Presidency of Gerald R. Ford; "A Time to Heal", the Autobiography of Gerald R. Ford.

Democrat James E. Carter, Jr.: 1977 – 1980

A former Governor of Georgia elected to the Presidency upon defeating Ford. Served in the Military.

'Jimmy' (as he preferred to be called) Carter, after a short honeymoon with the press very early in his administration, based on a fresh face 'outsider' with a reform message, came to be ridiculed as an idealistic, naive President who could do little that was right. Oddly, decades after his term, he has been enjoying wide coverage by the leftist major media, because of his access, outspokenness, and extremely pacifist, ultra-liberal views.

Carter aspired to make the Federal Government more compassionate, responsive, more efficient, and more people-oriented. With one brilliant exception – the Camp David accords between Egypt and Israel -- his administration's conduct of foreign policy was one blunder and setback after another.

His championship of human rights was exploited by the Soviet Union and other nations. He effectively 'gave away' the Panama Canal, established full, formal diplomatic relations with the People's Republic of China that compromised Taiwan, was naive in negotiations with the USSR over the nuclear limitation treaty, reached an accord with North Korea over weaponry that the latter violated.

Carter helped to effectively depose the Shah of Iran, a strong ally of America, and to usher in the anti-American theocracy that has reached increasing dangerous levels today. Carter was hapless in the face of Iran taking over and holding hostage the U.S. embassy staff – which led to foreign perceptions that America would not defend its honor or interests. Earlier, Carter directed clandestine military aid to Afghanistan; then he stood by as the Soviets invaded that country.

Some wags describe Carter as subscribing to policies characterized by such terms as 'speak softly and don't carry a stick', and his diplomacy by offering 'a carrot and then a bigger carrot'. In the National Archives' Presidential Materials covering administrations from Nixon's to Carter's (and up through Clinton's), along with interviews with Carter cabinet members and staffers including Zbigniew Brzezinski, Madeleine Albright, Leslie Denend, and William Odom, in the "Carter Presidency Project" of the Miller Center Foundation, these descriptions were borne out. Carter received a good deal of sympathy over his intentions and integrity, but was viewed as fundamentally weak, indecisive, failing to close ranks, and, unwilling to fight.

As examples, The Red Chinese leadership, in normalization talks, finessed the Carter people into agreeing that there was only one China; normalization talks with Vietnam also exploited the Carter administration flaws; and with Iran, Khomeini saw so much weakness in Washington, even when the theocracy was in its fragile early days, he called the administration a "headless chicken", because Carter and his emissaries went virtually begging for cooperation instead of using the threat of force (Amir Taheri, NY Post, Nov. 2, 2004).

These results were not from neglect. Carter was notorious for micromanaging many things – allegedly, he supervised the assignment of parking spaces at the White House -- including the day-to-day details of foreign policy. His own staffers viewed him, expressed after his administration ended, as indecisive, not forceful, and overly focused on his human rights agenda. As an incentive for better USSR-USA relations, Carter contemplated the liberal licensing of American oil-production technology as a bargaining chip, in the context of 'economic diplomacy'. This was presumably a page from the Henry Kissinger 'book' of normalizing relationships to reap the consequent business opportunities.

The Soviets also exploited what they perceived to be an American weakness in the late 1970s by brazenly furnishing military equipment to its budding allies in Africa (e.g., Ethiopia) and the Middle East, to the point of flying over countries – Turkey, Iran, and Pakistan, without permission. They and other nations concluded that Carter was so obsessed with human rights he would view problems in that context instead of what they meant to American honor, influence, and security.

The failures over the Iranian hostage taking and a ludicrous rescue mission exemplified those weaknesses, and convinced latter-day terrorists and other entities inimical to America that they need not fear retaliation. [Years later, during the first bombing of the World Trade Center in 1993, that conclusion still held water, and in the interim, until and after 9/11/01 encouraged more acts against the U.S. by Islamic terrorists, which Carter hasn't condemned, except in qualified terms he regards as 'balanced'. In fact, he tends to blame America and American policies for terrorist actions]. The actions, inaction, and submissive posture conformed to a strategy developed by Carter's National Security Advisor Brzezinski, who felt the U.S. and its allies could not contain the expansionist policies of the Soviet Union.

Accordingly, the strategy called for the creation of Islamic allies that for religious and political reasons would prefer America to the 'godless' Soviet empire, and, to encourage revolt by the Muslim minorities in the Soviet Union itself. The denial of the Shah's visa to come to New York for desperately needed medical treatment exemplified the strategy as did the coddling of the mullahs. Tactically (and familiarly) , the Carter administration took the position of voluntarily apologizing for 'American mistakes' over history, when dealing with Iran and other nations.

Despite all these disastrous outcomes and failures, Carter continues to this day advocating appeasement to the enemies of America and its allies. He has abrogated the tradition of ex-Presidents not undercutting Presidents in office, particularly in foreign affairs. All in all, accordingly, historians have ranked him as among the poorest of all U.S. presidents, while a friendly media treats Carter as a statesman of note. Extremely opinionated, he regularly intrudes on current issues.

Primary Sources: The Jimmy Carter Library; Transcripts of the Miller Center Foundation; Benador Associates website.

Republican Ronald W. Reagan: 1981-1988

Elected to the Presidency over incumbent Carter in 1980; re-elected by a landslide in 1984. No military service.

The 'Great Communicator' is considered by historians to be a near-great former President, but is accorded a lesser status by the major media, despite significant popularity among the people. A successful strategy that led to the breakup of the former Soviet Union, along with solid economic growth, are the pillars of comparatively high status. In fact, his conduct of foreign policy had setbacks as well as triumphs.

A former actor and union official, Reagan evolved from a liberal to a doctrinaire conservative, and served two terms as Governor of California. He was swept into the Presidency in 1980, in part due to the failures of the Carter administration over the Iranian hostage situation, economic 'stagflation', along with a general malaise in the country.

A mainstay of his foreign policy was the buildup of America's defense forces and his emphasis on the use of technology to further that cause – to nullify nuclear weapons. He negotiated with the USSR carefully, stressing verification of nuclear arms reduction, rather than relying on goodwill or faith.

Reagan sent bombers against Libya after a terrorist incident against American soldiers in Berlin, used naval escorts to assure the free flow of precious oil from the Persian Gulf during the Iran-Iraq conflict, and, supported anti-Communist insurgencies in Central America, Asia, and Africa -- exemplified by aiding the Afghans against the Soviet Union, aid to Angola, and aid to Nicaragua. Reagan installed Pershing missiles in Europe, and invaded Grenada in the face of a communist threat.

He was an unremitting hawk for whom defeating the Soviet Union was the top priority, describing it as "an evil empire headed for the ash heap of history". The press treated him with disdain as a reckless 'cowboy' and warmonger. During his administrations there were many organized anti-war and anti-American demonstrations – to little avail vis-à-vis influencing policy.

Reagan increased the budget in support of the radical Muslim Mujahidin against a corrupt Afghanistan government allied with the Soviets, aided Pakistani military intelligence, and convinced the Saudis to support the Contras in Nicaragua. He also built up Saddam Hussein's regime in Iraq, to counter the Iranians. He did virtually nothing in response to the shooting down of Korean Air Lines plane KAO7, and, little in the face of Soviet cheating on arms control matters.

Reagan, on the other hand, learned that so-called anti-American demonstrations were contrived, and was not upset by them. He was also furious over the Carter betrayal of Taiwan, and promoted the US-Taiwan Relations Act to discourage Communist China adventurism. The Strategic Defense Initiative was a particularly bold stroke that would eventually cripple the Soviets. The idea was to convince the Soviets SDI was feasible, and, compel them to spend precious resources to stop it. This was buttressed by feeding and letting them 'steal' bad technology to further waste their time and resources, to hasten military economic bankruptcy – and it worked. This strategy effectively ended the Cold War.

On a smaller scale, the administration confronted an insurgency in El Salvador, mediated a peaceful settlement in Namibia in southern Africa, but failed to bolster the moderate, pro-western government in Lebanon, suffering the loss of 241 Marines in an unanswered terrorist bombing, and, was helpless in the Soviet suppression of the Solidarity labor movement in Poland. Reagan also has his record marred by the Iran-Contra arms scandal involving Nicaragua.

Reagan did establish strong relationships with Great Britain, France, and Germany, and attempted to build the basis for a fair settlement of the PLO-Israel conflict. He succeeded in reaching his main objective: winning the Cold War, which led to the breakup of the Soviet Union's 'Empire', and subsequently an era of peace, save for the ensuing global terrorism.

Primary Sources: The Ronald Reagan Library; Informed Comment of the Global Americana Institute, Aug. 2, 2005; Taped Interviews of former Reagan administration officials; From Revolution to Reconstruction, American History, 1990.

Republican George Herbert Walker Bush: 1989 – 1992

Reagan's Vice President was elected to the Presidency. Served in the Military.

George ("Poppy ") Bush was a moderate 'gentleman' and genuine war hero as a fighter pilot in the Navy during World War II. He had the misfortune to succeed Reagan, the literal 'tough act to follow', and he was viewed with skepticism by the Conservative Wing of his Party. He also was treated lukewarmly by much of the major media, which seemed ready to pounce on him at a moment's notice for a slip-up (for example, when he broke his pledge not to raise taxes during a brewing recession, and, when he was featured on the front pages of newspapers and main stories on television on the occasion of his taking ill and regurgitating during a state visit in Japan), and, which only gave him grudging credit for his successes. On two occasions, the attempted assassination and wounding of Reagan in 1981, and, a 1985 Reagan operation for colon cancer, Bush was a stand-in president.   A   great deal of history occurred during his watch – events that did not reflect the results of his own issues and ideology so much as his dealing with them based on experience, modesty, and character. His resume' for the presidency was impressive: Vice President, UN Ambassador, Envoy to China, Director of the Central Intelligence Agency, Chairman of the Republican National Committee, Congressman. However and typically, as described by a senior National Security Council official referring to Bush beyond the resume', it was said "there was no punch, no there there; no particular position or policy or thesis taken or shaped with conviction" (Miller Center of Public Affairs, George Bush: Featured Events, 2003).

In addition, a liberal journalist's essay on PBS labeled him as "preppy", suggesting to Conservatives that Bush did not take their causes with sufficient gravity (there also is broad agreement that Bush's raising of taxes in 1990 and neglect of the U.S. economy in 1990 and 1991 contributed significantly to his not being re-elected in 1992. Another factor was the presence of a third (anti-Bush) candidate, Ross Perot, which arguably pulled more potential votes away from Bush than from his opponent, Bill Clinton).

Though the collapse of the Soviet Union and attendant events, and the hugely successful 'First Gulf War" dominated the main points during the Bush administration, many other foreign policy events also occurred. The Marxist-led government of Nicaragua was defeated; Panamanian strongman Gen. Manuel Noriega was forced from power; support of South African reforms helped to end its policy of racial segregation; the Tiananmen Square uprising in China; summits with Soviet President Mikhail Gorbachev resulted in the signings of treaties on arms reduction and other matters; the last American hostages in Lebanon were freed; peace talks about a Middle East settlement between Israel and its Arab neighbors were orchestrated; a serious program to encourage export growth, especially to Asian nations, was launched; an Earth Summit was held in Brazil; a North American Free Trade Act was drafted. At one point after the Gulf War, Bush enjoyed a record 80% approval rating, for a while.

Vis-à-vis U.S. – Soviet Union matters, Poland rebelled successfully; the Berlin Wall fell and East and West Germany were soon to unify into one nation; communist governments collapsed all over Eastern Europe. During these events a number of summits were held with Soviet leader Gorbachev, the most vital of which was Bush's pledge not to exploit the freeing of the Soviets' Eastern European satellites. Gorbachev did not interfere with the collapse of the Berlin Wall, and Bush agreed not to go to Berlin to gloat over the victory. Arguably, these events were more the result of the Reagan strategy for winning the Cold War, than of Bush policies, and so the latter received relatively little credit for the resulting outcomes that occurred during the years of his own administration.

Iraq's invasion of Kuwait in August, 1990 – which was heartily supported by the Palestinians, particularly in Jordan, but, opposed by Syria, Saudi Arabia, and other

Arab nations, provided Bush with his most serious crisis and subsequently to his finest hour as President. Bush diplomacy fashioned a broad international coalition of 34 nations, including some of which were Arabic, against Iraq, and, also enjoyed UN support as well as broad public support in the U.S. The allied forces liberated Kuwait and then began to assault Iraq itself, bringing the latter to its knees. But, unexpectedly, Bush ordered a cease-fire before Iraqi dictator Saddam Hussein was ousted – an act Bush would later describe as "his biggest mistake"*.

Hussein exploited the situation to reassert his leadership, re-arm, attack the Shi'ites in the South and the Kurds in the North. He also did seek to obtain and develop and again use weapons of mass destruction, and step up his aid to terrorists. There was documentation of contacts between Iraq and the terrorist organization al Qaeda, which is still unaccepted by liberal politicians and many in the media. Eventually, these led to a second, more costly and more controversial Gulf War with Iraq in 2003, following the World Trade Center (WTC) attack. Bush's reluctance to 'finish the job' left problems to his successors.

Primary Sources: George Bush Presidential Library and Museum; Miller Center of Public Affairs, University of Virginia; Wikipedia, The Gulf War; Various accounts released during the succeeding administration.

* There was a great deal of rationalization for not overthrowing Hussein at the time of the first Gulf War. This emboldened Hussein. Bill Clinton failed to deal decisively with Iraq; subsequently, his successor, George W. Bush, took the U.S. to war with Iraq, ostensibly because of links to terrorists and a question of Weapons of Mass Destruction. That happened in 2003, and involved some of the same players of the first Bush administration. On his own part, George H.W.Bush, before admitting to his mistake, based on CIA reports, hoped Hussein would be overthrown in an internal coup. The senior Bush and his advisor Brent Scowcroft, as argued in their 1998 book, "A Wolrd Transformed", were concerned that continuing the offensive would have fractured the alliance and resulted in numerous, unnecessary human and political costs. A point also made was that the U.N. mandate was only to free Kuwait, and, was silent about invading Iraq. Then Secretary of Defense (and later Vice President in the 2001-2008 Bush administrations) Dick Cheney, supported the cease-fire, on the 'party line' grounds that otherwise the U.S. would have to occupy and govern Iraq, and keep troops there indefinitely. In the second Bush's administration, Vice President Cheney was a hawk who strongly supported the invasion of Iraq and the overthrow of Saddam Hussein. That very action was   overwhelmingly approved by both political parties in the Congress, following the World Trade Center and other attacks on American soil on September 11, 2001.

Democrat William Jefferson Clinton, 1993-2000

Then Governor of Arkansas, Clinton was elected President by plurality in a three-man race. He went on to serve another term as a result of another three-man race, in 1996. He was a draft-dodger.

Clinton, a multi-term Governor of Arkansas, was the third youngest President in history. He was a devoted anti-military figure, so much so he was a fugitive felon until pardoned by President Carter in 1977.

During his tenure in the White House, recurring scandal and controversy were commonplace. Those followed from his Arkansas days, and were the basis for his being called 'Slick Willie', a name he abhorred. To his credit, over the two terms there was a substantial turnaround of the U.S. economy, marked by budget surpluses and progress in other areas. A share of the credit appropriately belongs to the conservative Republicans, which took over control of the Congress in 1994, and worked up various reforms in compromises reached by the more liberal-centrist Clinton.

Clinton was apparently adored by foreign leaders, because he often acquiesced to their wishes instead of exercising American leadership.

But, with regard to foreign policy and activities or lack thereof, the Clinton tenure was dismal, at times literally bordering on treason, such as his arranging for military secrets to be made available to Red China. His legacy, characterized by inaction, deals, disingenuous spin, was primarily responsible for the advance of global terrorism and the events leading up to the '9/11' attacks on the WTC and the Pentagon. There also were unanswered terrorist attacks on other U.S. assets abroad.

Where President Nixon made foreign policy his own raison d'etre and gave domestic matters a 'back seat', Clinton's stance was the opposite. He had little interest in foreign matters, but, a keen interest in domestic affairs –principally based on the greater ability to exert some control over the latter. At root, however, the focus on domestic policy and decision-making was to burnish his image and grip on power, both of which were given much higher priority than the overall interests of the nation's defense and common good.

Arguably, Clinton was the most scholarly and intelligent of the modern Presidents, as well as a superb speechmaker. But his conduct was regularly and in retrospect marked by evasiveness, unwillingness to admit to error and to accept responsibility. He was a master at obstruction, evasion, procrastination, and disingenuousness.

Clinton was a rogue, a larger-than-life unique Presidential character. He was cherished by the major media, who were quite willing to overlook, excuse, or rationalize Clinton's excesses and dark past. In his second term he was impeached, but, survived the ordeal, given strong political support by Democrats and a handful of liberal Republicans. The major media treated the unfolding drama as a soap opera, actually demonizing his prosecutors and positioning Clinton as a victim.

The impeachment and the ongoing controversies seemingly from Day One and up to his last days in office, probably cost his Vice President, Al Gore, from succeeding to the Presidency. Gore lost to George W. Bush, Governor of Texas, in an extremely tight election. Arguably, just as President Ford was made to pay for Nixon's 'sins', Clinton's trans-gressions probably cost Gore the election.

William Jefferson Blithe, III's widowed mother married Roger Clinton, a substantial man who owned car dealerships, when Bill was 4-years old. Clinton the ever-politician would later state that he was raised in a humble background. He was formally adopted at 14.

Clinton attended Georgetown University in Washington, D.C, worked for Arkansas Senator J. William Fulbright, a foreign-relations 'heavyweight', and then won a pre-eminent Rhodes Scholarship to Oxford University in London. His political sympathies – and concern about his own 'skin' – led him to vigorously protest the U.S. involvement in Vietnam, and to avoid being drafted. While abroad he did a fair amount of travel, including time spent in Moscow.

Clinton went on to attend and graduate from the Yale Law School. Returning to Arkansas, he taught at the University, ran for and lost a race for a Congressional seat, and was later elected Attorney General.

In 1978 he was elected the state's Governor. Clinton made his 'splash' at the 1988 Democrat Convention, and, in 1992 successfully ran for President against the incumbent George H.W. Bush, with a plurality of the vote in a three-man race.

During the campaign and in the years that followed, issues arose, including the use of marijuana and cocaine, womanizing, the avoidance of military service, shady business deals, and more serious crimes, including accusations of rape and sex with an intern. He survived them all, save for a tattered reputation, being found guilty of perjury, and the loss of his lawyer's license.

Over his eight years in office there was one foreign policy blunder after another. Finding one brilliant policy gem that was positive for America's interests eluded this author, as well as Clinton's critics and some former members of his administrations. Clinton did play up the fact that he kept the country out of war during his terms as a counter to the succeeding Bush administration that went to war over Afghanistan and Iraq. However, the Congressional Research Service reported that military fatalities from all causes, including terrorist action, military action, accidents, were 14,107 during the eight Clinton years in office, and, 7,932 fatalities during the first seven years of the Bush administrations.

Shortly after taking office in 1991, Clinton was faced with an attack (there would be a second attack 10 years later) on the World Trade Center in New York City, resulting in seven deaths and over 1,000 injured. Clinton never visited the site, viewed the incident of foreign terrorists committing a war-like attack on American soil as a legal matter much of the ordinary criminal variety; he failed to take any real anti-terrorist action, nor any steps to construct a homeland defense to guard against future attacks.

In 1993 there was a terrorist attack on the CIA headquarters in Langley, Virginia, in which two Americans were killed and three were injured.

In 1995 the Murah Federal Building in Oklahoma City was bombed by domestic terrorists; 168 people were killed and over 800 injured. Subsequently, documents showed one of the terrorists, Terry Nichols, had met with a terrorist bomb expert, Hakin Murad, in Pakistan, which led to speculation about possible foreign involvement in the bombing.

As amply detailed and analyzed in investigative reporter Gerald Posner's book, "Why America Slept/The Failure to Prevent 9/11", at the core lay Clinton inaction against increasing terrorism, despite his 'tough' speeches and promises of action, to the contrary. In White House meetings led by Clinton, the emphases were on public relations -- protecting and advancing Clinton's image – rather than vigorous counter-terrorism. This posture and policy would be the priority and pattern throughout his presidency.

A number of Security, Investigative, and Intelligence officials, as well as White House aides, independently described Clinton as 'soft on terrorists', careless, disingenuous; they called him a 'frat boy', henpecked by his wife Hillary, who was primarily focused on 'spin' and fund-raising. They accused him of being unprincipled, dishonorable, self-indulgent, a 'knave' who put personal and political objectives ahead of everything else. At one point Clinton is said to have lost the codes used in conjunction with the 'nuclear football'.

During the sex scandal with his intern Monica Lewinsky, took measures up directly with Russia and China; hat in hand, he asked the leaders of those nations for help in making him look like a statesman, to divert attention away from the unfolding scandal. At other times, he did take action on the foreign front, but none of it was decisive, strategic, or effective.

In fairness to Clinton, other Presidents as well as him, blurred the Constitution's explicit provisions about the respective roles of Congress and the Executive Branch during hostilities. The Constitution specifies that Congress and Congress alone decides declarations of war and when troops may be sent into combat. A President can act on his own in defense and in retaliation in the event of a surprise attack. The President is supposed to brief and consult with the Congress on such matters. The War Powers Act of 1973 mandated that a President had 90 days to obtain Congressional approval of a military action, otherwise the troops would have to come home. But, as to whether a Congress enforces the Constitution and Act depends on the particular Congress's resolve.

The Congress did not challenge Truman's sending troops to Korea. Reagan ignored the Congress in actions involving Grenada, Lebanon, Libya, Central America, and the Persion Gulf. Congress did not challenge President George H.W. Bush in actions in Panama and the first Gulf War.

In Clinton's case, he ignored the Congress when he took military action without overt provocation, such as retaliation for an attack or in defense. He just went ahead in Kosovo, Bosnia, Somalia, Haiti, and Iraq. Comparatively, Clinton choose politically safe, soft 'target' actions with appaent little military risk. Thus he could trumpet his 'strong posture' on military affairs. But, each of those paled in scale against the type of action Truman took in Korea. In point of fact, both Korea and Vietnam were undeclared wars. Clinton's own Secretary of State, lawyer Warren Christopher, testified that "Clinton did not care about foreign policy". He himself (Christopher) avoided fights (military action) at all costs. The pair's philosophy and practices emboldened terrorists and hostile states such as Iraq and Iran. Both men were inclined to pass the buck along to the United Nations to take action, as that largely impotent, politicized, and procrastinating organization would see fit.

Subsequently, recognizing the dangers of not taking action against terrorists, and in retaliation for the 9/11 attacks, and, over concern about weapons of mass destruction in the hands of enemies, Clinton's successor George W. Bush sought and obtained Congressional approval and some support from the U.N. However, after giving support, the Congressional Democrats turned tail and withdrew their support for the Iraq action; some even suggested that the basis for their original support before flip-flopping was based on incorrect information furnished by the White House.

Exemplifying inaction by the administration and the U.N., Clinton ignored the massacres going on in Rwanda; no troops were sent there, over one million lives were lost in internecine fighting. So much to the claim of helping African nations.

Nuclear accords were reached with North Korea, but the administration gave too much, asked little in return, and did not insist on verification. Two U.S. light-water reactors were supposed to be used for electricity; instead they were used for the processing of highly-enriched uranium for military weaponry. The Clinton administration chose to ignore the 'double cross', so as not to look as being 'taken in'. In 2002 North Korea blatantly announced its nuclear capabilities.

The administration supported a build-up of a militant Islamic base in Bosnia, which included fighters, intelligence assets, arms shipments, and political cover. That gave the terrorists a foothold in Europe, and resulted in massacres and terrorist activity. Priorities? Participation in an anti-terrorism summit in Egypt in 1996 was subordinated by Clinton, who took the occasion to lobby Russia to buy more frozen chicken from Arkansas. The administration also pressed for more favorable trade policies with the Peoples Republic of China, and, allowed China to take over both ends of the Panama Canal. In addition, several U.S. islands in the

Arctic were turned over to Russia, stripping people of their citizenship. A Russian spy ship operating in U.S. waters was covered up. The START pact was revised, which opened the door for Russia to export submarine missiles as space launchers, to China, Iran, and North Korea.

The administration boldly proclaimed America was safe from missile attacks, and used that specious argument to oppose the development of a long-range missile defense system. An anti-drug program designed to reduce the import of cocaine from Columbia was also undermined. Clinton desperately wanted to be seen as bringing peace to the Middle East. Israel was pressured into signing the Oslo accords with Palestine leader Arafat. Territory in the West Bank and in Gaza was relinquished, terrorist activity increased, despite Arafat's promise to curb terrorism against Israel. Later, Israeli Premier Ehud Barak was pressured by Clinton to give the Palestinians 91% of the land they desired and demanded, in exchange for another vague promise about halting terrorism and co-existing in peace. That generous offer was rejected by the greedy Arafat, who then launched the Intifada terrorist campaign.

Elsewhere in the Middle East, Saddam Hussein kicked out the U.N. weapons inspectors with impunity, and the administration simply stood by. That despite pronouncements by the Clinton administration that Iraq had weapons of mass destruction (WMD). Documents also showed links between Iraq and terrorist leader Osama bin Laden of al Qaeda. There was concern, but no action, over the possibility of Iraq furnishing terrorists with WMD.

In 1995 an al Qaeda terrorist attack in Riyadh, Saudi Arabia, killed five Americans and injured many others. In 1996 the Khobar Towers in Saudi Arabia were bombed, reportedly by Iranian-backed terrorists, and 19 Americans were killed and more injured. In 1998 the U.S. embassies in Kenya and Tanzania were bombed, resulting in 224 fatalities. In 2000 the U.S.S. Cole destroyer was attacked by a suicide bomber; 17 sailors died.

Clinton claimed that he made efforts to get and kill bin Laden, that it was a matter of the highest priority for quite some time. However, in his 1,000-plus page biography, "My Life", bin Laden is mentioned only once, after over 900 pages. Clinton also claimed his administration put together a plan to invade Afghanistan, topple the Taliban, and kill bin Laden, according to Michael Scheuer, who led the CIA's hunt for bin Laden.

Richard Clarke was Clinton's terrorism czar. He went on record as saying Clinton did not want bin Laden assassinated – a matter confirmed and reconfirmed in books such as "Losing bin Laden", and by Clinton aides Mansoor Ijaz and Dick Morris. Not only did Clinton pass up a number of opportunities to get bin Laden, on one occasion the al Qaeda leader was tipped off by a chain with a Clinton security aide at one end, who in turn informed Pakistan intelligence, which was sympathetic to bin Laden, and who gave the warning minutes before the attack. A few years later Clarke turned against the Bush administration over WMD and related matters pertaining to Iraq.

At the very end of his administration, in exchange for funding and political leverage, Clinton pardoned scores of criminals, including the FALN Puerto Rican terrorists responsible for 130 bombing attacks in the U.S. that resulted in fatalities and extensive damage.

In what arguably is the most egregious actions of his Presidency, Clinton accepted covert, illegal campaign contributions from China, and, donations from greedy, unpatriotic defense companies seeking sales and profit – even at risk to America – from business in China. In exchange the Peoples Republic received open access to the designs and test results of every nuclear warhead in the U.S. arsenal, and, missile technology, capping a catalog of blunders and worse, vis-à- foreign policy and action.

To this day and undoubtedly beyond, Clinton remains a larger-than-life figure, still sought by a fawning media. His time is spent spinning his legacy, still positioning for center stage, still hustling, and showing none of the traditional retirement modes of earlier Presidents. In his attempt to enhance his wife Hillary's campaign for the Democrat Presidential nomination, which failed, Clinton saw a lessened devotion from the major media, as well as artful rejection by many Democrat office holders. That resulted in Barack Obama gaining the nomination.

Primary Sources: The William Jefferson Clinton Memorial Library; the Hudson Institute; the Congressional Research Service; the Center for Advanced Study of Leadership and the Fulbright Intelligence Center, University of Maryland; the Ashbrook University Center for Public Affairs; the Centre for Research on Globalization; various National Security Council, FBI, and CIA records and testimony by officials; NewsMax, various journalists and authors including J. Michael Waller, Ken Timmerman, Richard Miniter; Cal Thomas,

David Plotz, Stan Roth, Col. Eugene Holmes; Lt. Robert Patterson.

Author's Note: In conclusion, it became apparent that Truman and Reagan were the most successful foreign policy Presidents of modern times, especially in the sense of defending America against America against its enemies and in meeting challenges.

On the other hand, Presidents George H.W. Bush, Dwight D. Eisenhower, and even Richard M. Nixon, strictly in the context of foreign policy, had net average success.

As for the others, President Lyndon B. Johnson showed his lack of executive experience and abilities – his long suit was legislation. John F. Kennedy was an inexperienced, over-his-head, casual, dangerous and indecisive President, but, he was patriotic. Gerald R. Ford was a weak President who accomplished very little.

James E. Carter, though sincere and principled and well intended, was a naïve, impotent fool who played into the hands of the enemies of the United States, and left office with a host of strategic problems for his successors. Finally, William Jefferson Clinton, with one foreign policy failure after another, also came very close to being a modern Benedict Arnold, willing to sell out his country for his political and personal purposes.